Own Your Future

Straight Talk about How to Buy a Business and Build Your Future

Bill Grunau

iUniverse, Inc.
New York   Bloomington

Own Your Future
Straight Talk about Buying a Business and Building Your Future

iUniverse books may be ordered through booksellers or by contacting:

iUniverse
1663 Liberty Drive
Bloomington, IN 47403
www.iuniverse.com
1-800-Authors (1-800-288-4677)

ISBN: 978-0-595-52040-4 (pbk)
ISBN: 978-0-595-51561-5 (cloth)
ISBN: 978-0-595-62123-1 (ebk)

Printed in the United States of America

iUniverse rev. date: 3/3/2009

Dedication

To the three people I hold closest in my heart: Cerisa, Ryan, and Brittany, who have always loved me, always believed in me, and remain the core of my life. I have learned much from all of them and they have added so much to my life.

Contents

List of Illustrations and Tables

Foreword

Buying a business and becoming a business owner is an aspiration shared by many. The question is where do you start, how do you find the right business, how do you finance it, and what steps do you take to achieve this goal?

Bill's book is a refreshing and knowledgeable approach to these and many more important topics as it relates to the acquisition of a business. His pragmatic and straightforward style gets right to the point, revealing the inner workings of how deals really get done.

First-time buyers, experienced entrepreneurs, and those that have dreamed of buying a business will find this book both informational and inspirational. This step-by-step guide is a must read for anyone interested in buying a business and will be a handy reference guide for even the most experienced entrepreneur.

Peter King
CEO, VR Business Brokers/M&A
and
JoAnn Lombardi
President VR Business Brokers/
M&A

Preface

I have seen many would-be entrepreneurs look for a business to buy without success. Some get very close and never close a deal; others never get beyond the looking stage; and many never really get started. In working with buyers who successfully bought businesses and countless buyers who did not, I found all had one thing in common—they had no idea how to go about buying a business. The fearless dove in thinking they would figure it out along the way, the methodical did their research and then moved forward, and far too many just got stuck or lost along the way.

While a number of books have been written about buying a business, I have found that none dig into the real how-to aspect, leaving the reader wondering where to start and what to do next. I have written this book with the new entrepreneur and first-time buyer in mind. It is intended to be a hands-on guide to get you started on your journey and guide you along your way to the successful purchase of your first business.

About the Author

Bill started working at thirteen and worked a variety of jobs through his teens; he joined the army at eighteen, and worked his way through college after completing his service. This was an unlikely beginning for a future high tech CEO. After college he started his professional career as an engineer and quickly worked his way up the corporate ladder to CEO. He became president of an electronics company at age thirty three. He's successfully turned around and repositioned many businesses, has been involved in both corporate acquisitions and divestitures.

He has been with VR Business Brokers since 2002, initially as a franchisee and now at the corporate office. During his tenure at VR he successfully concluded over fifty business sale transactions ranging from small to mid-sized privately held businesses.

Bill's career has spanned both big business, when he worked at publicly traded companies, and small business as both a small business executive and a broker selling small businesses. This broad background and eclectic experience gives him a unique perspective on business to draw upon.

Acknowledgments

I am truly blessed to have an amazing wife who has loved me for over twenty-eight years and continues to love me with her whole heart. Cerisa has supported and loved me through many ups and downs in our life, and through it all she remains my soul mate. We have grown together in so many ways. I am grateful we met, we loved, we lived, and we are still on our life and spiritual journey together. I have learned so much from her, she has added dimensions to my life that I would not have experienced without her. I am also blessed to have two wonderful children, now grown, who remain my closest friends. I am so proud of Ryan and Brittany, who have grown to be exceptional people.

Karl Fava, owner of Business Financial Consultants, our longtime friend and CPA, was kind enough to review and comment on parts of this book, ensuring that my financial facts are straight. I also persuaded Tom Lombardi, another longtime friend and a founding partner of Palmer, Lombardi, and Donohue, to review sections as well. Both Tom and Karl provided great suggestions and insight on some complex topics. I am grateful for their advice and longtime friendship. Steve Cooper was also kind enough to review the financing section to ensure that my facts were straight on the complex subject of using 401K/IRA funds to buy a business. I am also thankful that Steve Colburn of Eagle Capital, an expert in SBA financing, reviewed and provided comments on the SBA financing section.

Many friends in the business brokerage business have been mentors and shared their experience with me. Gary Hines, owner and broker of VR Business Brokers Newport Beach, was my mentor when I first entered this business. Gary spent many lunches with Cerisa and me, providing valuable advice, and became a good friend along the way. Ken Oppeltz, Bill Lange, and Steve Benson, all VR Business Brokers owners, also shared a great deal of advice when I first entered the business, and I want to thank them as well for their valuable advice and support.

Disclaimer

This book covers a complex subject, buying a business. There are many facets to buying a business, which include legal, financial, accounting, and tax issues. There is risk involved in buying a business; you should carefully consider these risks before purchasing a business. This book provides an informational overview of the steps involved in buying a business. The information in this book is based on the professional experience and opinions of the author. It is not a comprehensive treatment of the legal and financial aspects involved in buying a business. In chapter 7, "Picking My Team," I discuss picking your team of professional advisors, which include your attorney, CPA, and broker. While every effort has been made to make this book thorough, it does not replace the need for professional advice on legal and financial issues. The author strongly recommends you build a good professional team and use your attorney, CPA, and professional broker wisely. The author is not providing any legal, tax, accounting, or financial advice; you should seek advice in these areas from a qualified professional advisor.

Introduction

Owning your own business is rewarding both financially and personally. Buying a business is a challenging undertaking and a journey through territory you are likely unfamiliar with. My goal in this book is to provide you with a map to chart your course and the tools to navigate through this unfamiliar territory.

I have written this book as a hands-on guide for you to use in your search for a business. I recommend you read the entire text before you start your search and then refer to the chapters covering what you are involved in as you progress through your search and eventual purchase. The chapters follow your progress from preparing to start your search, to making an offer, to closing, and to becoming an owner. Chapters 1 and 2 provide some background and foundational information, and in chapter 3, "Build One, Buy One, or Buy a New Franchise," we get right into it. Buying a business is a complex task, and to do it right you need a team of experts to support you. In chapter 7, "Picking My Team," I discuss building your team of professionals to support you in the process. If you are purchasing a very small business, you may need only limited advice and support, while if you are acquiring a larger business, the transaction is more complex, and you will need good advice along the way from your team.

Businesses vary in both size and complexity, and the values of businesses vary widely. Regardless of the size of the business and transaction, the fundamental process remains largely the same. The exception to this of course is large M&A (merger and acquisition) transactions, which are handled by teams of investment bankers and attorneys and are beyond the scope of this book. Here we are focusing on small to midsize businesses and transactions.

Throughout this book, as I introduce new terms I will explain them. There are a few terms I would like to define now, as they are used throughout the book and from the outset. A list of definitions and terms is in the glossary at the back of this book.

Defining a few terms:

Buyer: The person buying the business or enterprise. In this case it is likely you.

Business broker or intermediary: Business brokers specialize in the sale of small to midsize businesses. Some states require a license to sell businesses, and some do not. I discuss business brokers in more detail in chapter 8 Working with Brokers. Many feel business brokers have developed a poor reputation over the years and some are now referring to themselves as intermediaries. I feel the term intermediary is less descriptive and a mouthful to say, so I have chosen to use the term business broker or broker throughout this book. I sincerely hope my friends in the business will not be offended.

Seller: The owner of the business who is considering selling it.

Discretionary earnings: Discretionary earnings are the owner's total economic benefit from owning the business. This includes the owner's salary, all other economic benefits, and perks. This is discussed in detail in chapter 10. For now it is sufficient to know that this is the owner's total compensation and benefit from owning the business.

Earnings: There are many different types of earnings that we will discuss in detail in chapter 10, "It's All about EARNINGS." Throughout the book, when I use the term "earnings," I am referring to the net profit of the business, including all the owner's economic benefits. This is called "discretionary earnings," or DE, which is the correct term, as earnings can mean several things.

The titles of some chapters have the word "My," "Me," or "I" in it. For example, "Does this Deal Work for Me" and "My 100-Day Plan." The context of "My" or "Me" is meant to be you. This is going to be *your* one-hundred-day plan, *your* deal, and *your* business, so the intent of these titles is for you to read it and own it.

Additional tools and resources are available at www.mybusinessbroker. com where you will find spreadsheets, examples, and other tools to make some of your work easier.

In some chapters I include success stories from actual past transactions. In these examples I have changed the names of the buyer, seller, and business to preserve their confidentiality. Throughout the book I use two hypothetical companies, Acme Industrial Distributors and Way High Manufacturing, to illustrate calculating the DE for a company, estimating the value, and determining whether the deal pencils out for you as a buyer. While both are fictitious companies, the figures are typical for the size and type of company used as an example, and both companies represent typical small business purchases.

I sincerely hope you find this book interesting, and more importantly a pragmatic and useful guide to successfully buying your business. I wish you the best of luck in your new venture, and my closing advice in this introduction is the following:

Though your journey may be long with challenges along the way, keep your destination (goal) in mind and remain focused on it. The course you plot today will likely change as you steer away from opportunities that do not work out and discover new opportunities along the way. Recognize this is a journey; it may have several unexpected course changes as you learn more and discover new opportunities. Enjoy it along the way.

Let's get started.

Chapter 1: Why Buy a Business?

Why buy a business? Everyone has his or her own reasons for buying a business. Many buyers are from the corporate workforce looking to replace a corporate job that was lost or is at risk, or to get out of an unfulfilling job. Others are looking for supplemental income or a business to replace the business they recently sold. Some just think it would be fun to own their own business and are fulfilling a lifelong dream. Some are driven by social causes and are social entrepreneurs with a desire to make money while doing a good thing, while others are intensely competitive and driven by a need to succeed. All entrepreneurs are driven by different motives, have their own unique ambitions, and their own view of what their business will be and how it will run. What they each have in common is that they are ambitious, driven, and fiercely independent.

Of course in addition to the personal reasons and satisfaction of owning a business, there are also great financial rewards from owning a business. Naturally you will receive income from operating the business. In addition, as you grow your business, the value of the business will increase, and when you sell it, you will benefit from your effort and investment. Unlike a job where you get paid every couple of weeks and when the money is gone that's it, owning a business allows you to build equity, the value of your investment in the business. When you sell it, you will get a nice bonus for your hard work and investment by converting that equity into cash. Later in chapter 21, "Exit Strategy," I will discuss how to develop an exit strategy to prepare to sell your business in the future and how to maximize the value of your business.

There are disadvantages to owning your own business too. Many owners become married to the business and end up working extra hours to achieve their goals and fulfill their dream. Most I have talked to don't mind the extra hours. They see it as an investment in their future. Unlike a corporate job where you work the extra hours essentially for free, as a business owner you are building your equity and your future. When you become a new business owner, the business will likely demand a great deal of your time in the first few months, perhaps the first year. It is important to have your family behind you when you start this journey. Over the long term it is important to balance your life so you don't put your family and personal life at risk and get burned out on the business in the process. Balancing work and the rest of your life is perhaps one of the biggest challenges in owning a business.

Family support can be a tough aspect of buying a business. It is important to have your family behind you when you start this journey. If your family is like most, everyone has a conventional job or corporate career. When you excitedly approach your family and friends with your "great idea" to go off and buy a business, don't expect them to jump up and down with excitement, and don't expect them to be enthusiastic supporters. Many of your friends and family will likely see this as a crazy idea, a risky venture, if not outright dangerous. Their concerns, which are really fears, are based on their personal experiences and limited knowledge. What is interesting about this is that in all likelihood none of them have owned a business, none have ever seriously looked into buying or owning a business, and none have any idea what the real risks and rewards are. To obtain their support you will need to educate them about the real facts of business ownership (in the next chapter we will dispel some myths about business failures) and demonstrate that you are going about this in a methodical manner, exploring a number of possibilities and doing your homework along the way. Even with this they may not be enthusiastic cheerleaders, but at least they will be cautiously supportive and won't be outright opposed to it.

Many people dream of buying a business, and that is as far as they go, just dreaming about it. Some tepidly take the first steps, become window shoppers, and never go beyond that. In the end only a small fraction of those dreaming of becoming entrepreneurs actually become business owners. What separates these dreamers from the successful buyers who become business owners?

Fear is perhaps the single biggest thing separating dreamers from owners. It would be easy to prescribe courage and say be brave, move forward in spite of your concerns and worries, and you will become a business owner. I feel this is shallow and naïve advice. To haphazardly jump into a purchase is silly and dangerous. What is the root cause of the fears buyers have? It is true some of their fear is about the risks of buying and owning a business, but much of their fear comes from the unknown. When an entrepreneur that is a first-time buyer starts looking for a business, little is known about what comes next and exactly how this is all going to come together. Not knowing the "how" in how to buy a business naturally causes a lot of anxiety and fear, and this stops many buyers from becoming owners; in fact it stops many from going beyond looking. Some other common worries buyers have are the fear of overpaying for the business, making a mistake (e.g., buying the wrong business, buying a bad business), and failing after buying the business. These fears often prevent buyers from actually writing an offer, and in some instances cause them to back out of a deal after writing an offer.

No book can eliminate fear; this requires action on your part. What this book will provide is the fundamental knowledge and basic principles of the "how" of how to buy a business, enabling you to take the first steps, then the next steps, and the next, and finally (with action on your part) successfully buy a business.

The stereotype for small businesses in most people's minds is that of a struggling small business owner barely paying the bills. True, there are lots of small and struggling businesses out there with little opportunity for growth. However, like all stereotypes, it is an unfair generalization that is not always accurate. The income from small and midsize businesses is as varied as the businesses themselves. Some very small businesses do have limited income, in the $40,000 to $60,000 range, while other businesses earn well into the mid six figures. Some even make over $1,000,000 per year, and you have the opportunity to own one.

In fact, by leveraging your cash as a down payment with bank and/or seller financing, you can buy a business valued at five times the cash you have available. For example, if you have $100,000 available, you can buy a business valued at $500,000 with bank (U.S. Small Business Administration, or SBA) financing. The best thing about leveraging is that the business pays off the debt while you are running it and have the income benefit of owning it. The business essentially pays for itself and even will repay your initial down payment investment! That's right. The loan payment check will come from the business every month and pay off the loan you took out to buy it and pay you a salary and other benefits along the way—a pretty good deal.

Some of you may be saying, well that's great; I don't have $100,000 sitting in my checking account. First, I have seen buyers buy a good small business with as little as $50,000 in cash. Secondly, you may have access to assets you are not even aware of that can be made liquid. For instance, your 401K/IRA or other retirement accounts can be rolled over into a new corporation owned by you to buy a business without paying taxes or penalties. You may also be able to use a home equity line of credit (HELOC) to fund your down payment or even your entire purchase. We will discuss this in detail in chapter 5, but for now let's leave it at there are numerous ways to fund your down payment and purchase.

Why are you thinking about buying a business? Are you fully committed to this? Are you ready for the challenges, work, and risks? Are you ready to take action? If you truly are committed to this, ready to get off the sidelines and jump in the game, and prepared for the challenges, then read on and let's get to it so you can *Own Your Future!*

Chapter 2: Myths and Facts about Small Businesses

It is a widely held belief that 80 percent (some even say 90 percent) of new businesses fail within the first five years.

Good news ... this is an urban myth.

- Fact: 50 percent of new businesses were still in business after four years, and 33 percent had failed.[2]

- Fact: Just 15 percent of new businesses that started with more than $50,000 of capital failed in the first four years.[2]

- Fact: 76 percent of the businesses operating in 1992 were still operating in 1996, and only 17 percent of the business closures, 4 percent of the total business population, were reported as bankruptcies or other failures.[11]

- Fact: The total number of business terminations (closures) in 2006 for businesses with employees was 9 percent of the business population, and bankruptcies accounted for only 3.6 percent of the terminations.[14]

Eighty percent of new businesses fail in the first five years; some even say 90 percent fail. I have heard this tossed out as a "fact" for many years, even believed it myself, and have seen it in print many times. While researching this book, I found some interesting data from the SBA and the United States Department of Labor. The SBA study "Redefining Business Success: Distinguishing Between Closure and Failure"[2] specifically looked at why new businesses closed and examined how many closures actually resulted from business failure. The study found that 50 percent of new businesses started were still in business four years later, and just 33 percent had closed as a result of the business being unsuccessful, dispelling the myth that 80 percent or even 90 percent fail. The other remaining closures were for other reasons, such as personal and sale of the business. Equally interesting, the study found that new businesses started with over $50,000 of capital and had just a 15 percent failure rate, while, not surprisingly, businesses started with no capital had a 45 percent failure rate.

According to the U.S. Department of Labor, 76 percent of all businesses in operation in 1992, including new and existing, were still in business in 1996. That's right. Only 24 percent were no longer in business. The report went on to state that only 17 percent of the small businesses that closed in 1997 were reported as bankruptcies or other failures. The other terminations were from the sale of the business, incorporation (sole proprietors forming corporations), or retirement of the owner. This would put the overall business failure rate at just 4 percent of the total business population. Recent data from the SBA and U.S. Census Bureau supports this as well. The SBA 2007 small business profile report lists 564,900 business terminations in 2006, 9 percent of the total business population with employees. Bankruptcies accounted for 19,700, or 3.6 percent, of the total terminations. In 2005, bankruptcies totaled 32,900, nearly double the 2006 figure, but still small in comparison to the overall business population. The report does not have details for the other terminations. It is also interesting to note that the 564,900 total terminations represent just 9 percent of the total business population of 6.1 million businesses with employees. It is very likely a number of small businesses did not declare bankruptcy and simply closed; regardless, the number of total terminations does not support the widely held myth that small businesses experience an extraordinarily high failure rate.

The 33 percent failure rate for new businesses reported in the SBA report still represents a substantial one out of three new business ventures failing.[2] It is interesting that this drops to 15 percent, or one out of six, for businesses started with more than $50,000 of capital. Although one out of three is substantial, it is a far cry from the myth of four out of five, or 80 percent of new businesses failing.

If we consider the risk of purchasing existing businesses, ownership risk drops substantially. Bankruptcies and business failures are reported as just 3.6 percent of the terminations, and overall business terminations (for all reasons, including sale, transfer, and personal) are just 9 percent of the total business population.

So while it is a myth that 80 percent of new businesses fail, it is a fact that a new business is eight times more likely to fail than an existing business.

More interesting facts about businesses and entrepreneurs in the United States:

- 79 percent generate less than $1 million in sales.
- 94.9 percent generate less than $5 million in sales.

- 89.5 percent have fewer than twenty employees.

- 98 percent have fewer than one hundred employees.

- 50.9 percent of the private sector workforce is employed by the small-business sector.

- 50.7 percent of the nonfarm gross domestic product (GDP) is generated by the small-business sector.

- 99.9 percent are classified as small businesses (the SBA classifies businesses with fewer than five hundred employees as small businesses).

- There are six million employer firms (businesses with employees who are paid a wage, also known as "W2 employees") in the United States.

- There are twenty-six million firms (employer and non-employer businesses) in the United States.

- 7 percent of the working age population is actively involved in efforts to start a business.

- There are 1.7 to 2 million businesses for sale at any given time.

Wow! If people ever doubted that the small business sector drives our economy, this certainly would change their mind. It is startling how big the small business sector really is in the United States.

It is also interesting to note that the data is only for firms with employees. In other words, companies with no employees are not included in these figures; if they were, the population of small businesses would be much higher. Of the more than 25 million businesses listed in the Census Bureau small business report for 2005 (the latest report available with detailed employee counts), six million had employees (employees are defined as persons paid a wage by the employer). The SBA small business profile report for 2007 (data from 2005 and 2006) lists 26.8 million total businesses, and 6.1 million firms with employees.

New Business Success & Failure after 4 Years

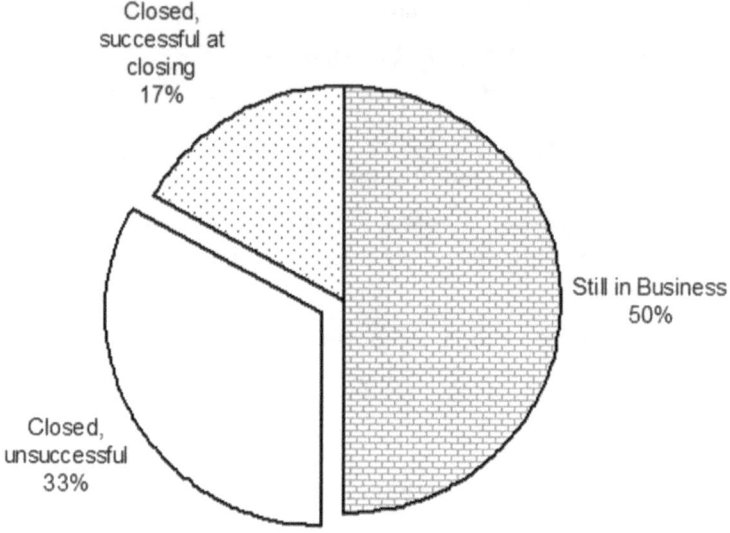

Closed,
successful at
closing
17%

Still in Business
50%

Closed,
unsuccessful
33%

2006 Business Terminations & Bankruptcies

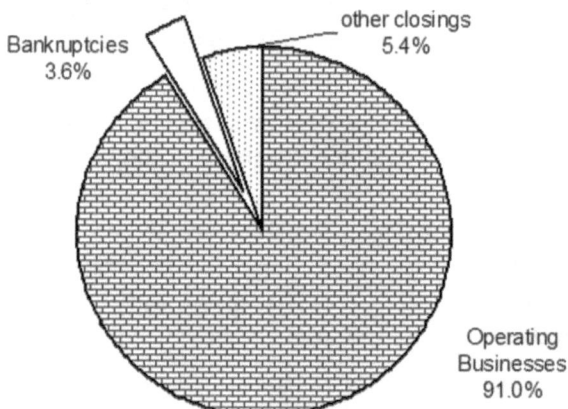

Bankruptcies
3.6%

other closings
5.4%

Operating
Businesses
91.0%

US Businesses with W2 Employees

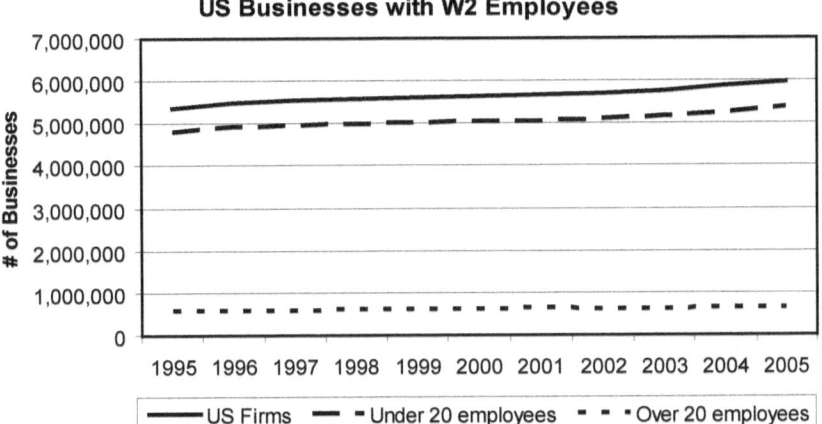

US Business Population by Sales

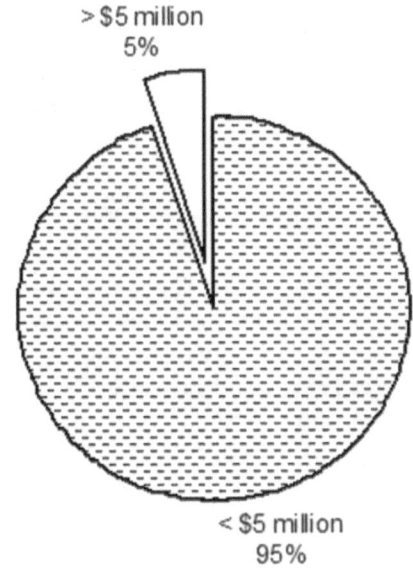

Chapter 3: Build One, Buy One, or Buy a New Franchise?

Should I build a business, buy one, or buy a new franchise? This is a question many entrepreneurs wrestle with. Let's take a look at all three choices.

Build One

An obvious question is why not start my own business? After looking at the asking prices of businesses you are interested in, on the surface it probably looks like you could start your own for less money. When all of the costs are considered, it is much less expensive to buy an existing business than it is to open and build one from the ground up, not to mention the risk factor. Opening your own new business may seem simple enough: find a location, get a lease, get the equipment, put up a sign, advertise, and off you go. You are in business, and the sales will take off. Like the line in the movie *Field of Dreams*, "If you build it, he will come." Or in your case, if you build it, the customers will come. Right? Well, people may come, but it will take time and money to build a new business from scratch. As the new owner, you will need working capital (more on this in chapter 5) to support the negative cash flow until the business grows and becomes profitable, which may take a long time, and probably much longer than you expect. If just the opening expenses are considered, you may be able to open your own business on a limited budget, but when all of the expenses are considered, it is always less expensive to buy an existing business, and certainly less risky. As discussed in the previous chapter, new businesses have an overall failure rate of 33 percent, and even new businesses with more than $50,000 of capital invested have a failure rate of 15 percent, which is two to three times the failure rate of ongoing businesses.

In case you still aren't convinced, let's talk about those other expenses. In addition to the money invested in start-up costs just to get the doors open, once the doors actually do open, you will be paying all of the operating expenses, such as payroll, rent, utilities, inventory, materials and supplies, and advertising. And your sales on day one will be ... you fill in the blank. But suffice to say sales will be slow when you first open, and they will grow slowly as you build your customer base and brand recognition. In fact, you will likely decide to spend more than you budgeted on advertising to get sales jump started, which is a good idea; but remember that is another up-front expense before the sales and cash flow are coming in, and it will eat into your working capital.

Buy One

A second alternative is to buy an existing business. When you buy an existing business, you will have cash flow from day one, assuming you bought a profitable business (more on this later). The business will be up and running, the customer base will be in place, inventory should be in stock, the facilities are built, and everything is ready to go. In fact, if the business has been running for some time now, it should be stable. This is a huge advantage over starting a new business from scratch, where it would most likely take months or longer to get to breakeven.

Another advantage, in fact a big advantage, to buying a business is that you may be able to finance a large part of the purchase. If the business you purchase meets specific minimum financial criteria and has good books and records, it will qualify for an SBA loan. With SBA financing, you will be able to finance up to 80 percent of the purchase (in some cases more, but 80 percent is the most common "loan to value," or LTV). For example, if you had $100,000 for a down payment, with SBA financing you could purchase a $500,000 business. This is discussed in detail in chapter 5.

There is seldom a true turnkey business or a "perfect business." Every business you look at will have something that can be done better, maybe many things that can be done better. The owner has set up the business the way her or she likes it and is comfortable with it. It is a personal choice. After all, the owner owns the business, so the owner can do it his or her way. If you buy it, you can change it to run your way, make all the improvements you want, and make it a better business. It is important to have reasonable expectations when you are looking for a business, as all of them will have some things that could be done better. I discuss this in more detail in chapter 4, "Is There a Perfect Business?" While there aren't any perfect businesses, there are always some very good ones for sale. It will take time to find the good ones, and you may look at a number of businesses with some real challenges. However, it is well worth the time and effort when you find the right one.

Buy a New Franchise

What about buying a new franchise? They have brand recognition, sales should start up faster, and cash flow would come faster. Wouldn't that be less expensive than buying an existing business? Not necessarily. While a good franchise will have brand recognition and will attract customers more easily than a new, independent brand, it still takes time, and the start-up expense is still substantial. Lots of franchise businesses are for sale as re-sales, and some of these are good deals; in fact, often you can buy an existing franchise for less money than the cost (when all expenses are considered) of opening a new one. It is true some established franchise units sell for large premiums. Even in this case I would argue that they are well worth the money. Franchise units selling for high earnings multiples usually have very high sales, great earnings, a well-trained staff, and a big brand name. All things considered, it is well worth the premium.

Bottom line, buying and opening a new franchise unit is much like buying a new home. The first owner has the expense of landscaping, decorating, window treatments, painting, and all the nice amenities the builder offers, like granite counter tops and premium floor coverings. The first owner may even add a pool, barbeque, and patio. The owner will get to enjoy having the home done exactly the way they want it. When the owner goes to sell the house, all of these things do add to the "marketability" of the house, but how much value do they add? Let's use the pool as an example. A $20,000 to $50,000 investment adds $5,000 to $10,000 to the market value of the home. Ditto for the other amenities. They may make the home more attractive to buyers, but they don't add much value, and you will never get that money you invested out of it. A home loaded with amenities is only worth a few thousand dollars more than the same model with just the basics. The same holds for opening a new franchise unit. You will invest heavily in building out the store or unit, building the business, etc. You will have the benefit of owning the franchise unit you wanted, where you wanted it, and set up the way you wanted it, and you will have the benefit of the cash flow from it while you own it. In the end, the value of the business is driven by the cash flow it is generating, end of story. No matter how nice the business is, earnings drive value (more on this in chapter 10).

So why would anyone open a new franchise? There are some instances where this makes complete sense. Let's face it: if you had an opportunity to open a McDonald's in a location where there was no other McDonald's for twenty miles, would you do it? Of course! Who wouldn't! Likewise, if you had the opportunity to buy a McDonald's in a great location that has been open for twenty years, and the price was a huge premium, would you be interested? Would this be a better deal than opening a brand new one? It may well be a better deal when all things are considered. If there is a particular franchise you are interested in and there are no stores or units in your area, then your only choice is to open a new one. If it is a strong brand with solid demand and need in your area, then it may be a great opportunity. So in some instances, opening a new franchise unit can be a great decision. It depends on your particular circumstances and what opportunities there are in your area.

Just to set things straight, I used McDonald's as an example because it is likely the best known franchise in the world, and everyone would want one. Before you run off to look for a McDonald's for sale, be aware that all of the major fast food franchisors require quick service restaurant (QSR), also known as "fast food," experience and will not even consider you for a new or existing franchise without it. Also, few of these mega brand franchises are for sale, and when they are, they are generally sold inside the chain to another operator. There is a growing trend with the large franchisors toward multi-unit operators, and the franchisor would prefer that an existing and successful franchisee buy a unit or units that are for sale. As a result, few of these ever hit the street.

There are thousands of franchise concepts available today. In fact, according to the International Franchise Association, in 2007 there were over six thousand franchise concepts (brands) available in the United States, and there were over seven hundred sixty thousand franchised units. Not all franchises are the same. The larger and more mature franchises have very strict minimum requirements for minimum net worth and liquid capital, and many require experience in their market (this is most common in the QSR market (also known as the fast food market). Some will not even accept new franchisees as single unit operators (e.g., you have to buy multiple units). There are many small franchises that are much easier to qualify and be approved for by the franchisor. While the small franchises are easy to qualify for, the earnings are typically much less than the big franchises, and much less than you would earn from the purchase of an existing business for an equivalent investment.

If you decide to buy a franchise, you should conduct your due diligence just like you would if you were buying a resale business. The franchisor is required to provide you with a franchise disclosure document (FDD), formerly called a franchise offering circular. The FDD is the franchisor's disclosure to you, the prospective franchisee, about the financial condition of the company (the franchisor), how many units are in the system, how many were closed last year and for what reason, how many were opened, and broad estimates of what your opening expenses would be. The FDD is reviewed and approved by some states and the Federal Trade Commission (FTC). It is important to remember that the agencies reviewing the document do not audit or verify all of the information. While it is illegal for a franchisor to lie in the FDD, most of the information is presented in the best possible way with the best possible spin on it. You need to carefully research and verify the information in the FDD, specifically the information relating to your opening costs and what the assumptions are in the estimates provided. You should then come up with your own estimate.

How much will I make from this franchise? The FTC considers any estimate or projection of earnings for a new franchise unit to be an "earnings claim" by the franchisor. As a result, few franchisors make an "earnings claim" in their FDD, as there is tremendous liability for them if they do. The absence of an earnings claim is not a red flag; it just means they are being conservative and careful, and have a good attorney. What is an earnings claim? Pretty much any estimate or statement relating to gross sales or profits, including averages from existing units, can be construed to be an earnings claim. Consequently, it is unlikely you will even get a verbal estimate from a franchisor as to what to expect for your first year's sales or profits. In fact, if a franchise sales person is making verbal earnings claims, make sure these same figures are in the FDD and they can back them up. If they can't, you should be very careful about using that figure.

So how do you do your due diligence and work up an estimate for your first year budget if you can't get these figures? You can extract some information from the FDD, and you can also contact existing franchisees and ask them. You will find some franchisees will be very open and helpful, and others will not. They are independent business owners and under no obligation to provide you with any information, so it just depends on the personality of who you reach. Although it may be hard to extract this information, I highly recommend talking to several existing franchisees as part of your due diligence before you move forward with your purchase of the franchise.

I have summarized some of the steps in buying a new franchise. If you decide to buy a new franchise or are seriously considering it, I highly recommend you purchase a book specifically on franchises and buying a franchise. You can find more information on franchises and a consumer guide to franchises[12] at www.ftc.gov, the FTC Web site. You can also visit the International Franchise Association Web site, www.franchise.org, which has a very good consumer guide[3] to buying a franchise, as well as a very good page of frequently asked questions on franchise businesses.

Below is a summary of how building, buying, or opening a new franchise compares to each other.

Comparison of Building, Buying, or Franchise			
	Build a Business	Buy a Business	New Franchise
Time to Profitability	1 year or more	Immediate	Months to 1 year
Risk	High	Low, depends on the quality of business	Low to Moderate
Financing	None other than your personal credit	SBA if qualified and/or Seller	SBA on some, equipment leasing on others
Choices	You pick what you want and get to do it your way	Lots of choices, limited to what is for sale when you are looking	Thousands of franchises, depends on what is available in your area
Resale Value	Depends on profitability & sales	Depends on profitability & sales	High for major brand franchises with good cash flow, modest for smaller franchises, depends on profitability
Marketability when you Sell	Depends on profitability	Depends on profitability	Higher than independent

Chapter 4: Is There a Perfect Business?

Are you looking for that "perfect" business, a turnkey operation ready for you to take over a business with excellent books and records, easy to run, well-trained employees, solid sales and earnings, and a great track record? If you are looking for that "perfect" business, I am sorry to disappoint you, but it does not exist. Every business, even very good ones, have problems, things that could be done better, opportunities for growth that have not been seized, books and records that could be better, and so on.

In fact, if you found a perfect business you may not want to buy it. Think about it. If the business were perfect, it would be at its maximum potential. There would be no opportunities for further growth (they have already been tapped), and no opportunities for improved profits (it is already operating at peak efficiency). You may not even want to pay the price for it, as the owner would likely want a high premium for such a gem!

Seriously though, there are no perfect businesses. Even the really good ones have room for improvement, with new ideas, new products or services, and new ways of doing things. That is where you come in! That is your opportunity and where your rewards will come from.

So if there are no *perfect* businesses, what does a good business look like? The definition of a good business is different for everyone. Consequently you need to give some thought to what is really important to you, what is an absolute must in a business, what is somewhat important, and what things you can live with if they aren't perfect. For example, if you have a strong sales background and are comfortable acting as the salesperson or sales manager at the business you buy, a business with great products and a weak sales force, or maybe no sales force (the owner is doing it himself), would be a good prospect for you, while another person without sales experience would consider it a weak prospect. To illustrate another example, if you have technical or engineering experience, you would likely be comfortable acquiring a manufacturing or technical company where the owner is heavily involved in the day-to-day operations and you would have to replace him, while someone with no technical experience would consider this too risky or too complex to take on.

Does this mean you should focus exclusively on businesses in your particular area of expertise? No, not at all. In fact, by focusing your search too narrowly, you will find few businesses to look at and may never buy a business. Although it seems logical to focus on businesses that can draw on your expertise and thus provide you with your best bet for success and the lowest risk, you should expand your search into other areas. While you may be thinking, "but I've been doing this for years, I am really good at it, and I like it," your skills and expertise are transferrable into other markets and businesses. You will be surprised at how much fun some of these new enterprises can be.

Let's take a look at a couple of success stories.

Retail Product Manager Buys a Commercial Cleaning Company

John worked as a product manager in the food industry. He had great sales and retail experience; he also had excellent management skills, and was in a good financial position (he had cash for a down payment and a good credit score). John wasn't really sure what kind of business he wanted; he just wanted a business that would replace his corporate job and comfortably support his wife and five children. John kept his mind open and was willing to look at a variety of different types of businesses, as long as they met his income requirements.

John successfully bought an apartment cleaning and painting company. As it turned out, he had some janitorial experience from when he was in college. Although the company he bought was very profitable and growing, it lacked a sales force (his strength), and the owner had pretty much "checked out," as he was bored with the company after starting it and owning it for thirteen years. John bought the company and successfully grew it 30 percent in the first twelve months. When he initially started looking for a business to buy, cleaning companies were not even on his list.

Was this a perfect business? Not a chance. It was a good business, very profitable, and had a lot of opportunity for growth, but it had its problems too. The previous owner was pretty much an absentee owner and was not around much. After John bought the company, he found out the office manager was embezzling by steering orders through a company she secretly owned. He estimates she was siphoning off nearly $60,000 a year this way.

There were other challenges too. John grew the company so quickly he was strapped for working capital (cash). Some of you might wonder how this can happen, but actually it is quite simple. He was growing so quickly that his labor and material costs were growing more quickly than the cash was coming in, because the jobs are invoiced net thirty days, so he had to wait thirty to sixty days before he got paid. Although growing too fast is a great problem to have, it was a challenge he had to deal with, which he did.

John's is a great success story. He grew the business, caught the thief, and increased his cash flow further. He now has a thriving business.

Warehouse Worker Buys a Retail Fitness Business

Robert worked as a warehouse worker, and his wife Susan worked in sales. They were looking for a business that would allow Robert to quit his job, work full-time in the business, and generate enough income to replace his current salary. They had great credit, a great attitude, and very limited funds for a down payment. They bought a local retail fitness business that sold treadmills, home gyms, and other fitness equipment. Although they had no retail experience and no previous experience selling fitness equipment, in addition to their great attitude, they had good sales skills and a willingness to learn the business.

What is interesting about this is that many other buyers looked at this business, and all passed on it. In fact, this business was on the market for three years with two different brokers! Many buyers felt the seven-day-a-week schedule was too much work. Others didn't think they could learn how to sell fitness equipment. And others were worried about competition from the retail giants like Wal-Mart and Costco. A few were really concerned about the fact the business was on the market for so long (What was wrong with it?).

Robert got a great deal on this business. It was priced very reasonably, excellent financing was available because the business had solid earnings and a great track record (in business for over eleven years), and most importantly, it was in his price range. In the end, he got in for a very small down payment with SBA and seller financing (we will learn about this in chapter 5), and he loves the business.

Were there challenges? Of course there were. Robert and the seller had some disagreements during training, and the seller was not as available as he had committed to be for training. Just before closing, a major supplier notified Robert they would not allow his store to continue to carry their product line anymore because they were going to use a different distribution channel strategy. Translation. They were going to give the product line to a competitor. This product line represented well over 30 percent of Robert's business, so this was a significant issue to be addressed. If it could not be resolved, the deal would die.

In the end, Robert and the seller found a new product line, with more products and better margins. Robert got through the training, albeit not with as much help from the seller as he had counted on. Years later Robert still owns the business, has hired a part-time person to work on his days off, and is doing well.

The bottom line is—there are no "perfect businesses." If you want to be successful in your search for a business, you need to open up your search and purchase criteria and be flexible in your expectations of what the business will be. In other words, if you keep your mind and your options open, like John and Robert did, you may find a great business in a market or industry you had not initially considered.

Chapter 5: Financing My Purchase: Where Do I Get the Money?

Financing is critical to your successful purchase. With financing you are a player, without it you are a spectator. What do I mean by financing? If you are purchasing a very small business, for let's say $100,000 or less, then by financing I mean cash, regardless of where you are obtaining it from. Few banks will finance the purchase of a business this small, although you may be able to get other bank financing, such as a HELOC or other personal line of credit. For transactions over $100,000, I am referring to your complete financing package: cash, plus bank financing, plus seller financing.

Some of you may say, "I have cash, so I don't need financing." Of course you could choose to make your purchase with all cash, but the question is why? Take a lesson from the private equity groups. They have hundreds of millions of dollars of cash and are capable of doing lots of deals with cash, yet they still leverage every deal and inject as little cash as possible into each deal. Why do they do this? The answer is probably obvious at this point. They can do more deals! With a 10 percent down payment and 90 percent financing, they can do ten deals with the same amount of cash. Yet there is a better reason to leverage your cash.

You are not likely to be doing multiple deals like the private equity groups, yet you should still consider using bank financing if you can. Why? You can go after bigger game! Let's take a look at a simplified example.

Lets' say you have $100,000 of cash. What are your options? Let's take a look.

Scenario 1: Buy a Business for Cash

Under this scenario you have $100,000, and you are going to buy a business valued at $100,000. As we will learn in chapter 11, earnings drive value. For this example, let's say the business you are buying is a small business and is priced at 2.2 X DE, which by the way is the overall average multiple for small businesses. That means you would expect to earn around $45,000 a year from your $100,000 investment. There is no debt service, so basically you can expect to get just less than half of your down payment back in the form of annual earnings.

Let's see what happens if we leverage our cash with bank financing.

Scenario 2: $100,000 down payment Plus SBA Financing

Under this scenario, the $100,000 is your down payment. If the bank agrees to finance 80 percent of the purchase price (80 percent LTV), that means your $100,000 is your 20 percent down payment, and the bank will provide up to $400,000 of financing for a qualified business. Under this scenario, you can buy a $500,000 business. How much would you likely make from this business? Again, let's work backwards from the valuation multiples, and let's assume since this is a bigger business it will be priced at a higher DE multiple. For this example, let's assume it is priced at 3 X DE (much higher than the example above, and actually a premium for this size business; but let's use it anyway). If the business is priced at $500,000 with a multiple of 3 X DE, then the DE is $166,667 per year, which is over three times the DE of the business in Scenario 1.

Before you get too excited, remember this is before debt service. So let's do a quick estimate of your net after debt service. Will you still make more money after you pay the bank?

In this example, you have a $400,000 loan, amortized (spread) over ten years. Interest rates vary depending on the prime rate. For this example, let's use 9 percent (you will have to check with your bank for current rates). A $400,000 loan at 9 percent interest fully amortized over ten years will have a monthly payment of $5,067, or $60,804 yearly. Subtracting the debt service from the DE, we wind up with $105,862, which is just over double the net earnings from Scenario 1. Remember we priced this business a bit higher, using 3 X DE here, and 2.2 X DE in Scenario 1, so we can afford to pay a premium and still make more money. Now do you see why leveraging is so attractive? But wait, there's more! Let's look at one other scenario.

Financing Comparison	Scenario 1: Cash Purchase	Scenario 2: Cash + SBA Financing
Down Payment	$100,000	$100,000
Bank/SBA Financing Amount: 80% LTV (Loan to Value)	0	$400,000
Purchase Price	$100,000	500,000
Discretionary Earnings (DE) Multiple	2.2	3.0
Estimated Discretionary Earnings (DE)	$45,455	$166,667
Monthly loan payment, 9% interest, 120 month SBA 7a Loan.	$0	$5,067
Annual Loan Payment	0	$60,804
Annual Net After Debt Service	$45,455	$105,862
Earnings Ratio: Cash vs. Leveraged	1	2.3 X Cash Deal

Note: This example is simplified and does not include loan points or closing costs. It is also assumed that both the business and buyer will qualify for SBA financing.

There is also a third option. What if you persuaded the seller to carry a note (seller financing)?

If the seller carried a note for, say, 50 percent of the purchase price, at 8 percent interest, for sixty months (these are typical terms for a seller note), then you could purchase a business valued at $200,000 with your $100,000 down payment. In this example your net after debt service would be $65,577, assuming you paid the same earnings multiple of 2.2 X DE. So a seller note for 50 percent of the purchase price increased your net after debt service by over $21,000, a 60 percent increase in your net with the same down payment.

The lesson here is that leveraging your cash really increases your earnings, and with financing you can afford to buy a larger and higher quality business.

An advantage to SBA financing is that it becomes a cash transaction to the seller and reduces or eliminates the need for a seller note. This can become a very useful bargaining chip for you when you make your offer.

Down Payment

The down payment for your purchase cannot be financed, at least not through a bank, and typically not through the seller. If you are tight on cash, you can get it from family and friends, borrow it before you go to the bank, look at smaller businesses, or wait until you have sufficient cash.

Why is it important to tap any sources of credit for cash before you submit your loan application to the bank? When you approach a bank for an SBA loan, the bank is going to look at your assets (things you own) and your liabilities (all of your debts, including credit cards, mortgage, and cars). The bank will make its decision to lend to you based on your credit rating, net assets, and collateral. If you approach a bank, submit your financial information, and then go back and borrow against your home (e.g., a HELOC), your financial position has changed dramatically, and it may cause the bank to reject your final approval (they don't like surprises like that). If you need to borrow any funds for your down payment, do it before you submit your application; but before you do any additional borrowing, make sure you will still qualify for the loan. It is best to talk informally with prospective banks to find out where you stand and what they require before you do any additional borrowing. Taking on too much additional debt for your down payment may disqualify you for the loan.

SBA Financing

First, let's clarify one thing. The SBA is not a bank; it is a guarantor that guarantees the loan. The bank you are working with is the lender; the SBA provides guarantees to banks making business loans to encourage banks to participate in small business financing and to provide liquidity to the market. The SBA charges the bank a fee or points for doing this, which is passed on to you. The points you pay go to the SBA guaranty fund to pay for defaults.

Nearly any bank you ask will say they do SBA lending. Some are better than others, some are more flexible on the deal, and some are inept at this type of loan. Make sure you use a "preferred lender" with a dedicated SBA lending group specializing in SBA loans. (I strongly recommend against using a retail banking branch for your SBA loan, since this type of bank is not as well equipped to handle SBA loans.) Also, make sure you can sit face to face with the bank representative who will be handling your file. I strongly recommend against using a lender where your contact will be a remote processing unit available only via an 800 number. Lastly, I have found that the best SBA lenders are smaller regional banks (again, make sure they are a preferred lender) and the big nationwide lenders that specialize in SBA lending nearly exclusively, like UPS Financial and CIT. These financial institutions are not retail banks. Their business is commercial lending, they specialize in it, and they are good at it. The nationwide SBA lenders have local representatives specializing in SBA loans who you can meet with face to face. Likewise a good local or regional bank with a dedicated SBA lending unit also will have an SBA lending specialist you can meet with face to face.

What's the difference between a preferred lender and any other bank offering SBA loans? A preferred lender has been approved by the SBA to do its own underwriting and does nearly all of the processing in-house, while other SBA lenders must submit the loan paperwork to the SBA for approval. Preferred lenders have much more control over the process and can approve a loan in-house, which means they can fund a loan much more quickly that other lenders. It also means there is less risk of the loan being rejected or being resubmitted several times. Using a preferred lender does not mean your loan request is a sure thing. The loan and the deal still must meet minimum financial ratios, and it has to make sense financially; but a good preferred lender has more latitude and can guide you through the process, and there is less risk of unpleasant surprises at the last minute.

There are two types of SBA loans[14], a "7a" and a "504." If you are buying a business, you will likely be getting a 7a loan, which is for a business acquisition. SBA 7a loans are amortized over seven to ten years; ten is the most common, with interest rates tied to the prime rate. The maximum interest rate (as of the writing of this book) is prime plus 2.75 percent for loans over seven years, and prime plus 2.25 percent for loans less than seven years. The bank does not have to charge the maximum amount. Depending on your loan and the current market conditions, you may be able to get a better rate. Again, it is important to shop around. You may find one bank charging the maximum rate and another willing to reduce it by as much as a half a point (e.g., from prime plus 2.75 percent to prime plus 2.25 percent).

SBA 504 loans are for real estate and capital equipment purchases. For real estate, a 504 loan can be amortized over twenty years with a much lower interest rate. Before you get excited and go looking for a 504 loan, remember this applies only to real estate. If you buy a business with real estate, you can use a 504 loan for the real estate part of the purchase, but a 7a loan must be used for the business acquisition. In the end, the two loans are blended or merged into one. The collateral for the 504 loan will be the real estate itself, and the 7a business acquisition loan may require additional collateral. Most businesses lease their premises, so it is likely if you are using SBA financing, it will be a 7a loan.

There is one other type of SBA loan called an Express loan, which is actually a form of 7a loan. The Express loan program was designed by the SBA to facilitate business loans for very small businesses and in some cases new businesses with little or no documentation such as financial statements for the business and a track record of earnings. Express loans are limited to three hundred fifty thousand dollars and are based primarily on the credit rating and credit worthiness of the buyer. Express loan fees allowed by the SBA are much lower than for the regular 7a loans and the SBA guaranty to the bank is also lower, so Express loans are not really a great deal for the bank and consequently most banks are not that interested in them.

The bank and SBA will require collateral, which means if you own a home with equity in it, real estate, or other assets, the bank is required to put a lien against this as collateral for your SBA loan. In some rare instances I have seen SBA loans approved without collateral, but it is very unusual. If you have a home or other assets, you will likely have to use them as collateral to get SBA financing. If you aren't willing to pledge your assets as collateral, then an SBA loan is not for you. Instead, you will have to do either a cash deal or one with seller financing only.

In general, the bank will ask for all of the collateral available. So if you have more than enough collateral to qualify, they may still "collateralize" (put a lien) on everything. There are some ways to minimize what the bank uses as collateral; however, you have to be careful, as it is a delicate balance. If you reduce your available collateral too far, you may no longer qualify for the loan. So, find out how much collateral is required to qualify for your loan before you take any action.

One way to reduce the available collateral on your home is to apply for a HELOC. Even if you do not use your HELOC, the equity in your home is reduced by the amount of the HELOC, which means the bank can put a lien on your home only for the remaining amount. If your home has less than 20 percent equity, the bank will not use it as collateral against your SBA loan. While this sounds like a great idea, it may cost you your loan approval if the bank isn't willing to do the loan without it as collateral.

Keep in mind that while the SBA lending rules are in the same for all banks, each bank has some latitude on how they underwrite and structure their deals. As a result, one bank may tell you no, while two others may be happy to do the deal. Likewise, one bank may want a lot of collateral, and another may require much less. There truly is a great deal of variation from bank to bank in this area, and it really pays for you to shop around.

Most SBA financing requires a minimum of a 15 percent to 25 percent down payment, with a 20 percent down payment being the most common. Some banks also like to see the seller carry a note as well, typically 10 percent to 20 percent of the purchase price. The bottom line is that if both you and the business qualify for SBA financing, you can finance from 75 to 85 percent of the purchase. Eighty percent is the most common.

Ask for a prequalification letter (many will provide this), and ask them to let you know the maximum loan amount you would qualify for. Few buyers walk in with a prequalification letter. When you have one you will stand out to both brokers and sellers as a serious, well-qualified, and well-prepared buyer. The bank is going to ask for a lot of details from you, starting with a personal financial statement, which will be on an SBA 413 form. You can download this form from your bank or the SBA Web site. It is handy to have a copy of your personal financial statement along with your prequalification letter, as some brokers and sellers may ask for this to ensure that you are financially qualified. Don't be afraid to go back to the bank if you find a great business that is just above your approval level.

Once you find a business and have an accepted offer, it is time to get to work with the bank. In the beginning, they want to see your personal financial statement, which is how they will qualify you. Once an offer is accepted, they are going to need lots of financial information about the business before you can get your approval. The basics are the last three years of tax returns, current profit and loss (P&L) and balance sheets, and a copy of the purchase offer. They will also ask for a business plan and other information. When you meet with your banker, find out what will be required. Most banks and brokers have a checklist they can give you.

Seller Financing

All sellers will say, "I am not going to carry a note." The reality is that most deals have some seller financing, and many smaller deals that do not qualify for SBA financing are financed by the seller, along with a larger down payment from the buyer. If the seller takes a firm position on this from the beginning, don't worry about it, and don't start negotiating this the first time you meet, or even the second or third time. It is very easy for a seller to say no to seller financing when you informally ask about it, and once a seller says no, it is more difficult to get to yes. You are more likely to get a yes when you present the seller with a written offer that includes seller financing as part of the deal.

If the seller is represented by a broker, you can privately ask the broker if the seller is open to seller financing.

When you put your offer together, remember the seller is not a bank, and the only collateral he is getting is the business itself. That's right. Seller financing typically has only the business as collateral. Additionally, if there is bank financing involved, the seller is behind the bank in priority, which means he or she is last in line to receive repayment. This makes some sellers uneasy, because regardless how good the business is, they have no control over it once they sell it, and they don't know who you are or if you are going to pay them. If you want to get seller financing, you have to sell the seller on you.

Typical terms for seller financing are five years and around 8 percent interest. While I say this is typical, seller financing is always a negotiating point, with the loan amount (note amount), interest rate, and note term (duration) all in play. All of these terms are negotiable, and to get the best deal, you may have to give on one point to get another. Ironically, deals are frequently lost over minor differences. I have seen buyers and sellers argue over the interest rate, sometimes arguing over one-half percent, and losing the deal over a very small amount of money because both wanted to win or have it his or her own way. So you may have to offer the seller a slightly higher interest rate or shorter term to get the price you want, or you might have to accept a counteroffer from the seller, with no seller note, to get the price you want. Remember, everything is in play. It is all negotiable.

Home Equity Line of Credit

During the real estate boom through 2006, HELOCs were a popular source of financing for business purchases. With home values soaring and home owner equity along with it, HELOCs were readily available for many home owners. Real estate values went flat in 2007 and have dropped in 2008 and 2009, which will lower available home equity and make HELOCs more difficult to obtain. Depending upon your home equity, a HELOC may or may not be a viable financing option.

HELOC rates and terms are generally lower than those for SBA loans, and the cost of financing a business purchase with a HELOC is much lower. If you can obtain a HELOC large enough for the purchase of your business, you will find that it is better than SBA financing. If you don't have enough equity in your home to cover the entire purchase, you can use a HELOC for your down payment, and SBA financing for the balance of the financing. Remember, from the section on SBA financing, if your lender requires a minimum amount of collateral, you want to make sure that any HELOC you obtain does not reduce your equity below the bank minimum.

Retirement Accounts without Penalties or Taxes!

Your 401K, IRA, or other qualified retirement accounts can be used to fund the down payment or purchase of a business. You may be thinking, well of course I can cash out the account, pay the taxes and penalties, and use my money, but who wants to do that! But wait; there is a way to use these funds without paying taxes or penalties. There are several companies that will set up a corporation so that the money from your retirement accounts can be invested into your new corporation and used for the purchase of a business. This is much like investing in a public company on the stock exchange, except the company your retirement account is investing in is yours. You run it, you control it, and you will determine how these funds are invested (which business you buy). This may sound like a simple self-directed IRA, and conceptually it is; however, there are substantial differences with respect to how it is implemented. The corporation, its profit-sharing plan, and retirement plans must be set up correctly with the correct documentation, and the transaction must be structured properly in order to meet Internal Revenue Service (IRS) requirements.

The above is a highly simplified explanation of this, and very strict IRS guidelines must be followed in order to qualify. The companies that specialize in this know how to correctly structure the new corporation, what documentation is required, and, most importantly, understand the rules and regulations that apply.

One company specializing in this type of transaction is SD Cooper Company, who was one of the pioneers in this area. They offer a plan called an Entrepreneur Rollover Stock Ownership Plan, or ERSOP^{tm}, which is an IRS tax-qualified profit-sharing plan where IRA/401K rollover money can be invested into the sponsoring business (the business you are buying). You (the entrepreneur) roll over your preexisting retirement funds into the new plan, and the money is used to purchase the stock of your new company. The acquisition of "qualifying employer securities" must be for "adequate consideration," which means the value must be reasonable (market value), and cannot be inflated or reduced. SD Cooper's Web site, www.ersop.com, has detailed information on how this works.

Friends and Family

Friends and family are another source of capital for a down payment or sometimes an outright purchase. Of course, this depends on your personal situation. If this is a possibility, it is another source of funds to consider and can be a way to come up with that extra cash you need for the down payment.

If you approach friends and family, remember they aren't going to be as excited as you are about this. In fact, they may think you are crazy. This is a normal response. They have not done the research you have done, they don't know the details, and they likely have never bought or owned a business before. They are likely thinking about the myth we discussed earlier that 80 percent of all businesses fail, and if this is true, this is a really risky proposition you are bringing them.

So don't expect them to be jumping up and down with excitement when you approach them with your "great idea." Go slow, show them you have done your homework, and walk them through the details if they are willing to listen.

How Much Do I Borrow?

In general I favor leveraging (borrowing) as much as possible, assuming the business can both support the debt service and provide sufficient cash flow for your needs (i.e., don't over borrow).

Why do I recommend this? After you have bought the business, or opened your new franchise or business, the banks will consider you a new business owner. This is true even if you purchase an existing business, because you will have new bank accounts and no history with the bank. Consequently, obtaining lines of credit will be difficult, and the bank will likely approve only very limited lines of credit until you have some history. If you preserve your liquid capital (cash) by leveraging (borrowing) more and minimize your down payment, you will have a larger cash reserve for working capital.

I also recommend you take a conservative approach to your borrowing. What I mean by this is that you should not use overly optimistic projections for your sales and cash flow. You should also have sufficient working capital and cash reserves set aside in case you experience any problems, such as a downturn in sales or some other unforeseen problem. If you leverage the transaction to the fullest, sinking all of your cash into the down payment (e.g., buy a business bigger than you can really afford) and closing costs, you will have no cash reserves left and a high debt service. So what happens if your largest customers start paying slowly or you have a slow month or two? You will be in big trouble. It is much like buying a house that is at the absolute maximum you can qualify for—one hiccup and you are in serious trouble.

Another way to improve your cash position is to purchase the accounts receivable (A/R), which are customers' unpaid invoices, if the company has A/R. Retail businesses seldom have any A/R because they are cash businesses, while business-to-business (B2B) companies almost always have A/R, since the products or services are sold to the customers on terms, typically due in thirty days. Some lenders will finance the purchase of the A/R because it is an asset. By purchasing the A/R, you will own these accounts and will realize the cash flow from them as the invoices are paid. If you do not purchase the A/R and are selling products or services on terms, you will not realize the cash flow from your business until the new invoices are due, typically thirty to sixty days after you have bought the business and closed escrow. So if you don't purchase the A/R, you will need extra working capital (cash) to pay the bills until the invoices from when you take over (your A/R) start getting paid.

The bottom line as to how much to borrow is this: plan on a 20 percent down payment if the business qualifies for an SBA loan, which means an 80 percent LTV. If you can borrow working capital and borrow to finance the A/R, it's a good idea to do this as well. If the business does not qualify for an SBA loan, then the only financing choices you have are cash, a seller note, and IRA/401K rollover funds. Before you move forward, plug these figures into the deal check worksheet and total cash requirements (TCRE) worksheet that can be found at www.mybusinessbroker.com to make sure it pencils out for you (e.g., you have enough cash to do it, and you are comfortable with the debt service and the net after debt service).

Let's take a look at a very interesting financing success story where the buyer used both SBA 7a and 504 financing and rolled over his 401K for the down payment.

Corporate Executive Finances 88 Percent & uses 401k for Down Payment

Jim was living in Colorado working as a district manager for an international electronics giant. In 2000 he was transferred to California to start up and head up a new division. With the 2001 downturn, the funding and interest evaporated for the new divisions, along with Jim's position. Jim was then offered a transfer to Southeast Asia that soon evaporated also.

In a fit of self-preservation, Jim's entrepreneurial spirit bloomed. Jim searched for a business to own, and online he found a specialty wholesale nursery out of state. The seller had a broker, and Jim engaged a local broker to represent him. The asking price was $2.5 million. An offer was made and accepted, due diligence commenced, some discrepancies were found, and negotiations ensued. The asking price of $2.05 million was agreed on, including land, the business, and the residence.

Then came the financing. Jim used $250,000 from his 401K and rolled it over into an ERSOP® Plan as the down payment on the business portion. The balance was funded through an SBA 7a loan. There was a 1031 exchange involved in the business property portion, and the balance for that was funded by an SBA 504 loan. The residential portion was handled with a conventional real estate loan.

It's been three and a half good years. Jim has retired the 7a loan, and one-third of the stock in the retirement plan has been repurchased.

Jim's goal is to divest the retirement plan investment in the business next year, and he has a good possibility of doing so. If so, he will have fully repaid his the 401K down payment investment in less than five years and paid off one of the SBA loans in three years.

This is a great example of financing! Jim used a variety of financing to buy a great business that would have been out of his reach with a conventional approach. In this particular instance, Jim was able to leverage this deal with nearly 90 percent financing. His down payment was only 12.5 percent, almost half the typical 20 percent down required, and he used his 401K funds for the down payment without penalties or taxes! Deals with financing like this are rare because most businesses do not have real estate included in the transaction (most businesses lease their premises), but they do happen. If the business performs strong enough financially and has good documentation, excellent financing is available.

Chapter 6: How Do I Find a Business to Buy?

At any given time there are between 1.7 and 2 million business for sale in the United States. Obviously, with a couple of million businesses for sale, there is one for you out there somewhere. The trick is finding it. Looking for a business is like looking for a job. You will likely surf through countless business listings just like surfing through the job postings, looking for opportunities that interest you and are in the right location. You will go out on lots of "interviews," in this case buyer–seller meetings, before you find the right one. Be persistent. This will take time, and you will likely look at many businesses before you find the right one. You will also likely make several offers before one is accepted.

Years ago most businesses for sale were advertised in the business opportunity section of the local newspaper. Today most businesses are advertised on "business for sale" Web sites. Businesses such as restaurants and retail stores are still advertised in the paper and are also advertised on the "business for sale" Internet sites. If you are looking for a small retail business, you can check the paper and the Web sites. If you are looking for other types of businesses and larger businesses, your search will be conducted primarily on the "business for sale" Web sites and through brokers.

You can search on a number of Web sites specializing in businesses for sale, and you can also work with a business broker. VR Business Brokers (sometimes referred to as simply "VR") has an excellent Web site, www.vrbusinessbrokers. com, with businesses for sale throughout the United States and in several other countries, and an international network of offices with well-trained professional intermediaries (brokers). You can also find nationwide listings of businesses for sale at www.bizbuysell.com and www.bizquest.com. Most of the listings on these sites are posted by business brokers. Working with brokers is discussed in more detail in chapter 8.

Many "business for sale" sites have a search feature where you can search for specific types of businesses in specific areas (e.g., cities or zip codes). It is tempting to set up a very specific search; however, if your search is too narrow, you may not find any businesses at all. When you do your searches, keep your search criteria broad. For example, instead of specifying a city, specify a county;

or in some cases go ahead and surf through listings in the entire state if you are looking at specific industries. It is best to search broad industry categories. If you specify a very narrow search, say sheet metal manufacturing, you could miss a great opportunity for a company that was classified as a distributor/wholesale company because it outsources its sheet metal manufacturing. Likewise, you may be surprised and find a really interesting company that is a great opportunity for you in an industry classification you would not have expected. So start with a broad search and surf through the listings. It is worth the extra effort. Most listings are from business brokers. New listings and changes are posted daily, so you should visit the sites once a week to look for new or changed listings.

Some sites allow you to set up a daily e-mail notification of new businesses for sale. For example, the VR Business Brokers Web site (*www. vrbusinessbrokers.com*) has a search engine on the site where you can set up your search criteria and also set up an e-mail notification of new businesses for sale. When you set up your e-mail notification, keep it fairly broad by specifying the county instead of the city, or even the entire state, and specify several broad industries, such as wholesale/distribution, business services, or manufacturing, as discussed above. The only categories you should exclude are those which you are either not qualified for, or have absolutely no interest in. Everything else should be on the table for consideration, at least for now. It costs you nothing to look, and who knows what you may miss by being too narrow in your search.

Almost all business sales are confidential. Accordingly, the ads on the Web sites are very general, with few details, and certainly no address or name for the business. This is done to ensure that the customers and employees do not find out the business is for sale. The summary or description of the business in the ad will be very broad as well, because if it is detailed and too specific, it will be obvious which local business it is. This frustrates buyers because they want to know more about the business, and it would be much easier if they could just click on a link and get all of the details. Of course, if you can do this, so can anyone else, including employees, customers, and suppliers. Then there is no confidentiality, so the owner may as well post a "For Sale" sign out front. So when you are looking at the ads, you must keep an open mind and recognize that the summary on the Web site is just that, a very broad overview of the business. Likewise, most sites post only the gross sales and DE, with no details on expenses and no P&L statement. As this is a public site, it would obviously be silly to post full P&L details here for the world to see, including your customers, employees, suppliers, and competitors. So when you are viewing the ads, recognize that they provide an intentionally broad overview of the business, with very little detail, to preserve the confidentiality of the sale. If the business looks somewhat interesting, pick up the phone and call the broker, or click on the link and send an e-mail to inquire about it.

When you contact a broker, he or she will be happy to have a brief conversation with you about the business and answer some general questions; however, the broker will not provide you with any details or confidential information, such as the business name, location, financial details, etc., until after you sign a confidentiality agreement. Depending on the broker and the size of the business, the broker may also require a personal financial statement at this time to ensure that you are financially capable and are qualified to pursue this transaction (confidentiality agreements and personal financial statements are discussed in more detail in chapter 8). After you sign the confidentiality agreement, the broker will send you a business profile that will have details about the business, typically including the business name, location, summarized financial information, and more details about the business itself. It is impossible at this point to determine whether the numbers are "real" for this business, or make any other decisions about the operations of the business. There just is not enough information at this point to decide whether this is the right business for you. To make that decision, you will have to go look at the business and meet the seller. It is impossible to properly evaluate a business over the Internet or by reading a business profile. If the business looks interesting, put it on your short list and set up a meeting. That is the only way to determine whether the business is a good prospect or not.

Some businesses start off overpriced (at the seller's insistence), and the price is reduced over time. You may see the same listing drop tens of thousands of dollars over a period of several weeks, or even months. Buyers often interpret this to mean there is something wrong with the business because nobody wants it and the price is being reduced because they can't sell it. While this could be true in some cases, most of the time it is really as simple as the business was overpriced to begin with, there was very little interest in it, the buyer traffic was slow, and finally the broker was able to convince the seller to reduce the price to get some inquiries coming in. A price reduction does not necessarily mean there is anything wrong with the business. It is just a price reduction. That's it. The only way to find out if something is wrong with the business is to pick up the phone, call the broker, sign the confidentiality agreement, and go look at the business if you are interested.

During the search stage you will be looking at lots of businesses, much like surfing through online job sites looking for a job, so it is important to get organized. Your first cut is fairly easy: eliminate the businesses that are of no interest to you, are substantially over priced (keep an open mind on some of these), or are in locations of no interest to you. As you sift through the prospects and narrow your list to a handful of interesting prospects, it will get progressively tougher to choose which ones to put on your short list, and then even harder to narrow it down to one or two. One way to organize your decision process is to use a scorecard to rate and rank each business. Below is an example of the business scorecard from www.mybusinessbroker.com. You can also create you own scorecard to evaluate the businesses you are looking at. The most important aspect of this is to be consistent in your evaluations, and use the same criteria for each business you consider so you can compare the scores later. The business scorecard example below shows three businesses that were evaluated. Out of a possible 100 points, business #1 was ranked at 60, business #2 was ranked at 78, and business #3 was ranked at 50. At this stage it is obvious that #3 will not make the short list, #2 is the leading prospect so far, and #1 is a possible backup.

Business Score Card

	Ideal = 5	Business #1	Business #2	Business #3
Sales & Marketing				
Customer Base (very small = 0, very broad =5)	5	3	4	1
Readily Available Market/potential for growth	5	5	3	2
Sales material	5	4	3	2
Financial Factors				
Seller's Discretionary Earnings (net income)	5	5	4	2
Earnings history (declining = 0, flat = 3, growth = 5)	5	5	3	2
Books & Records condition	5	3	4	3
A/R collection	5	3	4	3
Inventory (condition, value, etc.)	5	3	3	3
Working Capital Required (very high = 0, very low = 5)	5	1	4	4
Additional Investment Required? (high = 0, none = 5)	5	3	5	2
Risk	5	3	4	2
Deal Structure				
Financing (all cash = 0, good financing = 5)	5	2	5	4
Asking Price vs Value (is it a good deal?)	5	0	5	4
Non Compete & Training	5	4	4	3
Operational Factors				
Technical or highly specialized	5	1	4	3
Competititve position/quality of products & services	5	4	3	1
Staff & infrastructure	5	3	3	2
Personal Factors				
Location & operating hours	5	3	3	3
My ability to run the business	5	2	5	3
My confidence in the business itself	5	3	5	2
Total Score	100	60	78	51

Note: This business score card is for informational use and your personal evaluation of various businesses. It is not intended to replace due diligence or a comprehensive review of the business opportunities you may be considering. You should consult with your financial and legal advisors before making any purchase decision.

While these three businesses are hypothetical, let's take a look at why #2 is ranked higher. Although the earnings and growth of #2 were ranked lower than #1, the other fundamentals were ranked stronger, giving it a higher overall score. Of course, you could decide that the earnings and growth from #1 are still more important to you and that this outweighs the risk and increased investment, but if this were the case, why did you rank #1 and #2 the way you did relative to each other? This demonstrates the advantage of objectively ranking each business. There is much more to consider than just the earnings.

By ranking and keeping notes on the businesses you look at, you will be able to objectively compare the businesses later. You will be looking at a number of businesses, so I highly recommend printing a copy of the ad and business profile for each business for reference later. It is also helpful to set up a separate file for each prospect so you can keep all of your notes and information relating to each business in one place.

Your journey to "Own Your Future," owning your own business, has several steps, with each step including progressively more detail. It is tempting to take a short cut, skip a few steps, and get right into the details; however, this seldom works. In the early stages, you are doing broad searches and looking at a number of businesses. Next you get a bit more detail via the business profile, and as you narrow your list to a few prospects, you will meet with the sellers and get more detail. Finally you write an offer, and after it is accepted you start due diligence, which is where you have the opportunity to dig into as much detail as you like. You might ask, "Why can't I just get the details upfront?" In fact, this question is asked by buyers frequently. One problem with this is that it is just not possible to provide this level of detail to every buyer that inquires. Can you imagine providing a copy of tax returns, P&L statements, customer lists, etc., to everyone who inquired about a business, and then answering the barrage of questions resulting from this? The broker and seller would obviously not have enough time to do this for every buyer that inquired. And think about it, if you got all of this information for every business you looked at, you could never sift through it all anyway. It would be overwhelming. Another obvious problem is that this information is highly confidential, and the seller does not want to provide it to anyone until they have made an offer.

So the process has incremental steps, with increasing detail at each step. Jumping ahead a bit, one might ask, how do I make an offer before I see the books? This is explained in chapter 14, "Making an Offer"; for now understand that your offer is based on the information and claims made by the seller. Your offer will state that the seller represents that this information is true, and further your offer will have a due diligence contingency, where you have the opportunity to prove the seller's claims and figures to your satisfaction.

Steps to Finding Prospective Businesses

1. Search: Surfing the listing sites, look at a wide range of businesses; subscribe to the e-mail notifications for new businesses listed.

2. Contact broker and sign confidentiality agreement: Contact the broker on interesting businesses, and keep an open mind. Prematurely ruling out businesses limits your opportunities and choices; at this point you want to cast a wide net.

3. Review business profile: After you have signed the confidentiality agreement, the broker will send you the business profile. Though reviewing the profile will still not provide enough information to decide if you want to make an offer, it will provide enough information for you to decide whether this business is on your short list and whether you want to continue to the next steps.

4. Contact broker for more information: Contact the broker to ask questions about the profile. Get more information on the business, and set up a meeting with the seller if this business is still on your short list.

5. Seller meeting: This is discussed in chapter 9, "Working with Sellers." For now, it is sufficient to understand this is where you start looking seriously at a business and start getting into more detail. One word of caution: While you start getting into more detail at the seller meeting, this is not where you start asking the seller to prove his figures and to provide the tax returns and books for the business. That is done during due diligence, which is where you have the opportunity to review the businesses books and records. At this point your goal is to determine whether you are interested in the business and want to consider making an offer on the business.

6. Evaluate the businesses you are interested in: Let's say you find several businesses you are interested in. That's great; but how do you decide on one, or narrow the field to a couple? Use an evaluation chart to do a side-by-side comparison of the relative strengths and weaknesses of each business. You can download the business scorecard at www.mybusinessbroker.com

7. Write an offer: Writing an offer is a big step and a critical one. For now it is enough to know that this is your next step and the beginning of really rolling up your sleeves. I discuss writing your offer in chapter 14, "Making an Offer," and in the subsequent chapters we will discuss due diligence and the transaction process.

Obviously there are more steps after you write the offer. All of the steps to buying a business are outlined in chapter 17. For now, we are just focusing on the steps involved in finding a business and narrowing it down to a couple of prospects.

At this point in your journey, you have not selected a final destination (a particular business); rather, you are surveying your choices. Keep an open mind while you are looking at prospective businesses. If one looks interesting, go ahead and click on the link, or call the broker and ask for more information.

After checking it out, if it still looks interesting, move on to the next steps. If you find a few that you aren't sure about, go ahead and take a preliminary look. Remember, the information early on is summarized and does not tell the entire story about the business. You will look at a number of businesses that simply don't interest you, and it is easy to get impatient or discouraged after looking at several and finding nothing promising. Remember, there are nearly 2 million businesses for sale in the United States, thousands in your local area, and new ones coming on the market every day. It may take several months to find the right business for you. You will find one if you are persistent, open minded, and follow the steps outlined in this book. So, now you are ready to start your journey. Let's get to the next steps.

Chapter 7: Picking My Team

As a business owner, you are going to need a team. In fact, you will need your team in place before you buy a business. The team you assemble before buying a business will work along side you during the buying process as well as after you conclude the transaction and are a business owner. The obvious team members you will need are a certified public accountant (CPA) and an attorney; you will also need an insurance professional, a business broker (intermediary), and a banker. When you become very successful in the future, you may also need a tax attorney to advise you on investments and tax strategies.

First, let's talk about your broker. Your broker (or brokers, as you may work with more than one during your search), will be a key member of your team during the business buying process and thus your choice of a broker is critical. While you can start looking for your CPA and attorney before you are ready to start looking at businesses, it is not practical to start talking to and looking for brokers until you are actually ready to look at businesses. The best way to find a broker is to call on one of the businesses they are representing. When you are ready to start actively looking at businesses, you will run across a number of different brokers, as many of the businesses you inquire about will be represented by different brokers. Make sure the broker or brokers you are working with are full-time, professional brokers (intermediaries) who specialize in business sales and have a professional office they work from. Eventually, as you look at more and more businesses, you will get to know the active brokers in your area and will find one that you like working with. Your broker is paid by the seller when the transaction closes, so it costs you nothing to look at businesses. Even though as a buyer it costs you nothing to work with a broker, it is important to respect their time. If a broker thinks you are wasting their time, or are not a serious and qualified buyer, he or she will not want to work with you now or in the future.

When you are ready to start looking at businesses and searching for a broker, contact your local VR office as a starting point. VR's intermediaries are well-trained, full-time professionals who specialize in small to midsize business sales. An added benefit is that all of the VR offices are networked together and actively work with each other, which means your VR intermediary can help you with any listing in the VR network as well as with listings outside the network. You can find your closest VR office at www.vrbusinessbrokers.com and can also look for businesses for sale. When you find a business or businesses that you are interested in, call your local VR office to inquire about it, and follow the steps outlined in chapter 8, "Working with Brokers."

Next let's talk about selecting your CPA. The accountant you are using for your personal taxes may not be the best choice for your business team on this transaction, or even for the tax and accounting work on your business. Personal tax preparation is very different from small business accounting and business tax work. Make sure your accountant is a CPA and has business accounting as part of his or her practice. Also, ensure that your accountant is familiar with tax strategies for minimizing taxes on the sale of a business, and ask about the number of these transactions they have done. While you are at it, ask the CPA to explain to you the difference between a stock sale and an asset sale, and which transaction type is better for you when you are buying versus selling. This is discussed in more detail in chapter 13, "Stock vs. asset sale." For now, it is enough to know the answer is not the same for the buyer and seller; it seldom works to the advantage of both. This will give you an idea of how familiar the CPA is with these transactions, and you will get some free advice along the way. By the way, if the CPA says it doesn't really matter, continue to shop around and get some more advice.

Before you settle on your choice for a CPA, find out what the fees will be for preparing your taxes each year and what other services can be provided. I also recommend contacting a few of the CPA's current clients as referrals. Another thing to discuss with your prospective CPA is due diligence. You may want to use your CPA for some or all of your due diligence. Discuss due diligence with your CPA and find out how he or she can help you, what the range of costs will be, and whether you can save money by doing some of it yourself. Some CPAs are not particularly interested in due diligence work because it is very time consuming, and unless you are a client, it does not provide the CPA with recurring or long-term revenue The fact that your CPA is not interested in doing the due diligence work is not necessarily a red flag, because due diligence is a very small part of most CPAs' business and is not a focus of their practice.

When picking your attorney, the questions are similar. Attorneys tend to specialize in specific practice areas. When selecting an attorney, make sure the attorney has handled business sale transactions in the past and that this is an area of his or her current practice. Again, your personal attorney who prepared your will or trust may not be your best choice. Though you will need an attorney on your team, how much you use your attorney is up to you. It is easy to run up a sizable legal bill if you have your attorney review every document along the way. On the other hand, it would be foolish not to use an attorney at all. If your broker is using standard industry or trade association forms, you may be comfortable reviewing them yourself or with your broker. If the forms and agreements are what we call "in house" forms, developed by the broker's firm or attorney, or of more concern the seller's attorney, you may want to have your attorney review them.

Few banks build personal relationships with small businesses anymore. If you can build a personal relationship with your bank, that would be great. Even if you can't, you will need a bank to be your business bank where your business accounts, line of credit, and perhaps your SBA loan will be. Shop around for a bank that is both convenient and friendly to small business accounts. Take a look at the bank's charges and fees, since these can really add up on a monthly basis. Some banks are much more reasonable than others. Also ask about minimum balances and what happens if you are below the minimum balance. Inquire about deposits and whether they will put a hold on your deposits.

Your insurance professional is not directly involved in the transaction itself. In fact, you will not need the assistance of an insurance professional until you have made an offer on a specific business. Your insurance professional cannot provide you with quotes or estimates on your insurance until he or she knows your specific requirements and the type of company you are buying. You can wait to select your insurance professional until your offer has been accepted and you are in due diligence. At this point, you will have enough information to start shopping around for your insurance professional. I always recommend using the existing insurance company and broker as a starting point; likewise, I definitely recommend shopping around and comparing rates and coverage. Insurance is an often neglected area for small business owners. Many are underinsured, and many are overpaying because they don't bother to shop around and have become comfortable with the status quo. One thing to point out is that if you find insurance coverage for less money, you just got a raise, so to speak, since the savings will increase your earnings when you own a business; likewise, if it costs you more, your income just went down.

It's your team, you are the captain, and it's your job to lead. Your broker, attorney, and CPA are your key advisors, and you may get conflicting advice from them at times. Each has a different role and very different perspectives. Your CPA and attorney's job is to ensure that you get the best possible deal, that your risks are minimal, and that your terms are favorable. In some instances, they may get overzealous and take this too far, by being either too conservative on the deal or overly one-sided on the contract. By the nature of their job, they are risk averse and will always be conservative in their advice.

This can kill a deal and can also result in a large bill for professional fees if it gets out of control. Your broker, on the other hand, will be focusing on closing the deal, facilitating the negotiation of any issues that pop up, and keeping things moving along. He will be more aggressive in pushing the deal along. You can see the inherent conflict in your team. It is your job to keep things in check and balanced. In the end, it is your decision and your decision alone. They are your advisors and will not decide for you. As the team captain or manager, you will have to weigh their advice and make the final decision, which may mean overriding their advice at times.

As an example, a good friend of mine is our attorney. We have known each other for many years and have an excellent relationship. When we first met, he was reviewing a contract for me and doing a great job; he was very thorough. We sent our comments back to the other party, and then they sent their comments back. My attorney had more comments. As I said, he was being very thorough. Finally I asked him, what is the likelihood of these things happening, and he said it was small. He also told me it was his job to protect me and ensure that my risks were minimal. Rather than continue to play contract volleyball, I decided to go with the contract the way it was, as it was close enough to what I wanted, and the risks were minimal. So we closed the deal, and everything worked out fine. We saved a few weeks of contract volleyball and saved some money on our legal fees. My attorney was doing his job. It was my job to make the call that I was satisfied with the contract and could move forward. The point here is that a contract or a deal will never be perfect, and you can spend a lot of time and money playing contract volleyball. You have to make the call as to when you are satisfied.

I want to make a final note on your professionals, most notably your CPA and attorney. Every time you contact them or ask them for services, you will get billed. This is how they make their living, and if they are talking on the phone with you or meeting with you, they are not working on another project they can bill for. Therefore, they have to charge you for their time, or they are working for free. You can get a free initial consultation while you are choosing your team, but after that, expect to pay your way. It is in your best interest to use their time, and your money, wisely, and not to call them for minor things. Likewise you can save money by doing as much as possible on your own. With that said, it is far less expensive to pay for good advice than to make a bad decision without it. So if you need their advice, use them.

Chapter 8: Working with Brokers

Your broker, or intermediary, is a critical member of your team and will guide you through the process of finding and buying your business. It is important for you to develop a good relationship with your broker, as you will be relying on your broker for advice on a number of things, from deal structure and negotiations to financing. Your broker is much more than a salesman. A professional business broker or intermediary has been through extensive training on recasting financial statements and valuing businesses, negotiations, and deal structures; many have had advanced training on mergers and acquisitions (M&A), tax strategies, and structured sales. You will be relying on your broker's expertise in these areas, so it is important that you find a well-qualified professional broker to advise you.

Odds are, during your search for a business, you will be working with a broker or perhaps several brokers. There are many misconceptions on what the broker's role is in a transaction. This frequently frustrates buyers to no end, as they have unrealistic expectations of what the broker is going to do for them. Let's clarify what the broker's role is and how you can successfully work with brokers.

First, who does the broker really work for? The listing agent represents the seller and has a representation agreement with the seller, which means when the business sells he gets paid. The broker's commission is paid by the seller at the close of escrow, and most brokers only get paid if the transaction closes. Technically and legally, the broker is working for the seller and represents the seller. In "dual agency," where one broker represents both the buyer and seller, the broker has a fiduciary responsibility (that of a trusted advisor) to the seller and a duty of honest and fair dealing to the buyer. The legal language varies from state to state. The bottom line is that the broker is paid by the seller and has a higher duty to the seller to represent the seller's best financial interests. At the same time, the broker has a duty to be honest and fair to the buyer. Does this seem confusing? You bet it is. Brokers walk a tight rope in dual agency. Unlike residential real estate where it is common to have one realtor represent the seller and another represent the buyer, dual agency is far and away the most common form of representation in business sales. This bothers some buyers, as they feel they don't have anyone on their side. Think about it though. Even in residential real estate, when you have a buyer's agent, when do they get paid? It is the same as with dual agency—when the deal closes. So regardless of the legal definitions and language, and regardless of dual agency versus separate buyer and seller's agents, brokers get paid when a deal closes, and their primary goal is to close the deal. So in reality, everyone is really watching out for his or her own best interest. The seller and buyer have their own agendas, and the broker has his—close the deal. This actually can work well for you, as the broker wants this deal to close as much as you do. Understand this, and it can work to your advantage. If the broker knows you are a serious and well-qualified buyer, ready to do a deal, you will have the broker's attention.

If the broker is motivated to close the deal and the broker's primary loyalty is to the seller, does this mean you can't trust the broker? I personally know many brokers that operate with the highest integrity and do a great job of representing both buyers and sellers. If you are working with a professional broker, you can trust that broker to do his or her job with complete honesty and integrity. In fact, the broker has a legal obligation to do so. You cannot expect the broker to do your job and make your decisions for you. Only you can decide whether a particular business is right for you, whether it meets your individual needs, and most importantly, whether you will be capable of successfully running it. The broker can, however, tell you what he or she knows about the business, guide you through the transaction, help you get financing, advise you on deal structure, and facilitate the negotiations. Did you notice I said "facilitate" negotiations? The broker's job is to be an intermediary. By definition, the broker is not taking sides in this. Instead, the broker is there to facilitate the deal. You have the responsibility to make your own decisions, as does the seller.

Now that we have established the relationship between buyer, seller, and broker, let's take a look at how you can work with brokers to successfully find and buy a business (working with sellers is discussed in the next chapter). Brokers get dozens of phone calls every day from prospective buyers. Many buyers never buy a business; in fact, many buyers never even take the next step and go look at a business. This seems strange, but it is true. A large number of buyers never go beyond calling in and asking a few questions. As a result, brokers tend not to spend a great deal of time with prospective buyers when they call in. They get lots of these calls, and because most of them go nowhere, they want to be brief. When you call a broker for the first time, recognize that you are one of those calls and are not going to be a priority to him just yet. On that first call, respect the broker's time and be brief. If you are calling about a specific business, ask a few basic questions to see whether the business is a prospect for you. If it is, ask the broker to send you a confidentiality agreement, and then the business profile once you have signed the agreement. Brokers can spot a good buyer quickly. If you get straight to the point and know how the process works, you will stand out as a good buyer.

Let's talk about confidentiality agreements, since they are an important first step. All brokers will require you to sign a confidentiality agreement or nondisclosure agreement. These agreements will have much more in them than just confidentiality language. The agreement will certainly have non-circumvention language, which means you will work exclusively through the broker for this particular business, or for that matter, any business the broker introduces you to. Does this mean you are agreeing to work with only this broker for any business you look at? Most likely no; read the agreement carefully. It usually applies strictly to businesses represented by the broker and does not apply to other businesses. It may also have some language stating that if you and the seller circumvent the broker and conclude a transaction, you will owe the broker a commission. This is there to protect the broker in the event a seller and buyer have the bright idea to cut the broker out of the deal and save the commission. This is not a common occurrence, but it does happen, which explains why this language is there. Technically the seller owes the broker the commission, as he is the one who signed the representation agreement with the broker to sell the business. This is in your confidentiality agreement to ensure that the broker gets paid. There is no need to worry about it as long as you don't go behind the broker's back to buy the business. There will also be language stating that the broker has not verified any of the information from the seller and does not warranty or guaranty the accuracy of it. Again, this is common. It is put there to limit the broker's liability in the event the seller's information is incorrect or the buyer decides to sue the seller because he isn't happy with the way things turned out. Read the confidentiality agreement carefully. It is a legal document, and you will be signing and agreeing to the terms of this agreement if you want to work with this broker. Confidentiality agreements are not a negotiable document. The confidentiality agreement the broker uses is a standard form used by the broker's firm for all of the firm's clients, and it is not practical for the broker to negotiate this agreement with each buyer. If you aren't comfortable with the confidentiality agreement, ask your attorney to review it, or find another broker. While most confidentiality agreements are similar, they are not all identical. Some are more onerous than others. As you see more and more of these, you will recognize the language common to all of them and become more comfortable with them. There is one more thing—yes, you will have to sign a different confidentiality agreement with each and every broker you deal with. Each agreement is between you and that particular broker and does not apply to another broker.

So far it may sound like working with a broker is going to be tough. Not really. It can actually be a pleasant experience if you understand everyone's role and have realistic expectations. So what can you expect from a broker? Your broker is your advisor and deal facilitator. If you are interested in a business he is representing, he can give you an overview of the business, send you a business profile (after you have signed the confidentiality agreement), arrange a meeting with the seller, write an offer with you, facilitate negotiations, facilitate due diligence, and keep the closing on track. There is actually a lot the broker does behind the scenes to keep things on track. While the broker does all of these things, the broker does not make your decisions for you and does not do your due diligence (this would be an obvious conflict of interest, since the broker is paid when the deal closes). Likewise, most brokers will not search for prospective businesses for you. There are literally hundreds, possibly thousands, of businesses in your area that are for sale. It is impossible for a broker to look for businesses on your behalf. For one thing, the broker has no idea which businesses you are interested in and which you would pass on. Only you can make that judgment.

Buyers will sometimes ask a broker to "let me know if you see any good deals," or "call me if you find a good business for me." The broker has no idea what you would consider to be a "good deal" or a "good business," and as I said earlier, brokers get dozens of calls from prospective buyers every day. Once you develop a relationship with the broker or brokers you are working with, they will get to know what you are looking for. If you have demonstrated that you are a qualified and serious buyer, they will call you when something pops up.

Don't be offended if some brokers don't call you back. Many brokers are very bad about returning calls, and while I feel this is unprofessional and gives the profession a poor image, it does happen. If you are faced with this, follow up and send them an e-mail; many respond better to e-mail than to phone calls. The broker may not be calling you back because the business you are inquiring about already has an offer on it. Again, this is very unprofessional, but it does happen. If you find a particular broker is unresponsive or difficult to work with, look for another one. When you find one you work well with, ask if he or she is willing to represent you on businesses listed by other brokers. Most will say yes if you have demonstrated you are a serious buyer.

A good broker on your team will make your journey easier and help you reach your destination, successfully buying a business, much faster. You are the captain, and your broker is the navigator. Once you have chosen a destination (business), he will guide you through the process of buying your business. It may take some time to find the right broker and to develop a good working relationship, but this time and energy is a good investment. Having a good broker on your team will ensure your success.

7 Steps to Picking a Broker

1. Start by calling in about a business the broker has listed. Make sure it is a business you actually are interested in (remember the "time" thing). You can start by looking for businesses for sale at *www. vrbusinessbrokers.com*; *www.bizbuysell.com* and *www.bizquest.com* are also good sites and have a large number of listings available. Note that you may see the same businesses on all three sites. Many VR offices post on all three sites, and many independent brokers post on both BizBuySell and BizQuest.

2. Make sure the broker is a full-time professional business broker or intermediary and is not engaged in any other businesses (e.g., real estate sales, accounting, or other businesses). VR intermediaries are professionally trained and specialize in the sale of small to midsize businesses; your local VR office is a good starting point. You can find the closest VR office at *www.vrbusinessbrokers.com*.

3. Make sure the broker is operating from a professional office (e.g., not out of his or her home or a shared office. Note that all VR offices are in professional offices, and all VR intermediaries are full-time professionals).

4. Ask whether the broker has recast the financial statements for the business you are inquiring about, what financial statements were used (e.g., tax returns or P&Ls), and whether this is a task normally performed for his or her listings. If you are inquiring about a small retail business, there may not be recast financial statements, since many of these businesses do not have good records. The answer you are looking for from the broker is that he or she normally does this if the business has good books and records (financial statements).

5. Ask whether the broker has a business profile for the business. After you have signed a confidentiality agreement, the broker will send it to you. A professional broker will prepare a business profile for all of his or her listings. The amount of detail will vary greatly; small businesses will have a very brief profile, while larger ones will normally have a comprehensive business profile. At a minimum, the business profile

should give you an overview of the business, a financial summary, and some vital data, such as the number of employees, years in business, and products and services.

6. Ask whether the broker can refer you to an SBA lender that he or she has a good working relationship with (if you intend to or might use SBA financing). This will give you leads for potential SBA lenders.

7. And lastly, make sure you are comfortable working with the broker. Give this some time, as it takes time to develop trust and build a relationship.

10 Steps to Successfully Working with a Broker

1. Do your own searches for businesses for sale.

2. Respect the broker's time. Don't call until you have a business or businesses you are interested in, and don't call until you are ready to seriously start the process. Be brief on your first call. Ask only a few questions, and ask for the confidentiality agreement if you are interested in the business. The broker will send you the business profile with the details after you have signed the confidentiality agreement.

3. If the broker asks for your financial information, send it to him or her. Many brokers will want to verify your financial wherewithal before they send you details about the business. Have a personal financial statement ready to send. You can download a personal financial statement form at *www.mybusinessbroker.com,* or use the SBA 413 personal financial statement form available at *www.sba.gov.*

4. Get prequalified with an SBA lender if you intend to use bank financing (more on this in chapter 5, "Financing My Purchase: Where Do I Get the Money?").

5. Offer to come in to the broker's office and meet him or her. Note that some brokers will not want to meet with you until you are actually looking at a business (that "time" thing again). If this is the case, wait until you have found something and then offer to come in.

6. Build a cordial and professional relationship.

7. Ask your broker to walk you through the transaction process. This varies from state to state, as some states use escrows, and others use closing attorneys. This will prepare you for the process and also

give you an idea of how the broker works, which will help in your selection process.

8. After you have looked at some of the broker's businesses and have decided to use this broker, ask whether you can review the broker's purchase agreement and other forms. This will enable you to prepare in advance. Some of these agreements are a lot to digest all at once when you write an offer. It is much easier if you can look at them in advance. Also, you may decide to have your attorney review the forms if you are not comfortable with them or do not understand some of the language or terms.

9. Be responsive when you are working on a transaction. Respond promptly to counteroffers and other action items.

10. Be on time to all meetings with the sellers and your broker.

Chapter 9: Working with Sellers

First let's answer an obvious question. Why are the owners selling their business, or why do sellers sell? Are businesses for sale in trouble or struggling? Is there something wrong with the business? Most businesses are for sale for personal reasons, such as retirement, family or personal, or the owners are just tired of doing it after ten or fifteen years (also known as "burnout"). Surprisingly few are for sale for financial reasons, like cashing in or selling it at its peak value. Frankly, if the business is doing well and the owners are still enjoying it, it is not for sale, and if it were, the price would be far too high. Many businesses for sale are doing very well. As I said, the decision to sell is driven by personal reasons; it is just time for them to move on. Some businesses are for sale because the owners are struggling or are not doing well. These businesses are riskier than a business that is doing well; consequently, they are generally discounted and can be picked up for a bargain. Of course, as the old adage goes, "you get what you pay for," and businesses are no different. During your buyer–seller meeting, you will have the opportunity to ask the sellers why they are selling and to learn more about the business.

Sellers will meet with a parade of buyers while their business is on the market. Initially they are impressed with the traffic and are flattered that people are interested in their business. Eventually they get worn out after answering the same questions over and over again during buyer–seller meetings. Your first meeting with the seller will be the first time you actually see the business. You will have a long list of questions, and you will genuinely be excited to be there. For the sellers, you may be the fifth or sixth or even tenth buyer they have met, and your questions will likely be almost exactly what the last five or six buyers asked, which becomes redundant for the sellers. This is a very important meeting for you and the sellers. Obviously you need to get your questions answered and learn everything you can about the business; the problem is, the sellers are getting burned out on meeting with buyers and nothing coming from it. Some sellers handle this better than others, but every seller is different. Seller burnout on buyer meetings is a reality you must be prepared to deal with.

Although you are the buyer, the best way to view seller meetings is like a job interview. Yes, you are the buyer, but this is not Nordstrom (a fashion specialty retailer). The seller is not there to wait on you, and he is not going to be a salesman and "sell" you on the business. Business owners, sellers, are fiercely independent; that's why they own their own business. Consequently, some may come off arrogant or disinterested in buyer meetings, and this often gives buyers the wrong impression. The seller thinks this is a great business and doesn't understand why someone hasn't already bought it. Sometimes sellers are a bit insulted by some of the questions that are asked by prospective buyers, and as I said, all of them get tired of answering the same questions over and over again.

So how do you extract information from the seller? First, take just a few minutes and let them know a little about you. Sellers don't want your life story, and they don't really care about your corporate career; just give them the highlights, and most importantly, let them know you are financially qualified. If you have a prequalification letter from the bank, this is a great time to show it to them. Let them know you are a serious buyer, are interested in their business, and are prepared to do a deal if you like the business and it meets your requirements. Let them know what interests you about the business (e.g., why you are looking at it); this flatters them and lets them know you are serious. If you are looking at several businesses, do not share this with them. Some buyers think this puts them in a position of strength by saying, "I am looking at a number of businesses right now, so why should I buy yours?" or something to that effect. What the seller hears is that you are just shopping, have no idea what you want, and really aren't serious about his business; he immediately loses interest in you. Treat this like a job interview; you want to win the seller over, even if you aren't sure you are going to buy the business. Can you imagine how a job interview would go if your greeting was, "I am interviewing with a number of companies, why should I work for yours"? I suspect the interview would be over shortly. It is similar with sellers; if a buyer comes off as arrogant or if it is apparent the buyer is just shopping around and not serious about the business, why waste time with him. So your first step is to sell the seller on you as a serious and qualified buyer. Then you will have the seller's attention, and it will be much easier to get information from them now and work with them later. Remember, if you do buy the seller's business, this meeting is going to be the foundation of your relationship with the seller. It is very important for the seller to like you, trust you, and respect you.

Sellers want a motivated and serious buyer, just like you want a serious and motivated seller. They want to sell their business to someone who will take good care of it and be successful with it. Remember, this is their business; they have spent years building it, and they are very proud of it. They want the deal to go smoothly with minimum turbulence, and most importantly, they want the deal to close. By keeping this in mind when you first meet the seller and are while you are working with the seller, you will develop a better relationship that will pay you dividends and help you close the deal.

Some Tips on Your First Buyer–Seller Meeting

1. Get as much information as possible from the broker before the meeting. This saves a great deal of time, and you will arrive better prepared.

2. Focus on key questions important to understanding the business.

3. Keep your questions straightforward and to the point.

4. Don't get bogged down in details in the first meeting. You can drill down into more detail later; first determine whether you are even interested in the business.

5. If it becomes obvious that you are not interested in the business, politely conclude the meeting and save everyone, including yourself, a lot of time. I have seen buyers continue on in excruciating detail only to tell me later they knew early on it was not for them.

6. Meeting times: Most sellers want to meet after hours to preserve confidentiality and to ensure that the employees do not find out the business is for sale. It is absolutely critical you respect and honor your confidentiality agreement and do not visit the business during business hours, unless the seller has specifically agreed to it. If you do visit during business hours, with the seller's permission, make sure you maintain the confidentiality of the prospective sale of the business and do not discuss it with any employees or customers. Visits during business hours are typically for retail businesses, and the prospective buyer visits as an ordinary customer. Meetings for B2B businesses are almost always held after hours or on weekends when the business is closed. Never call the business or visit the business without contacting the broker or seller in advance. Always arrange all meetings and handle all contact with the seller through the broker.

A few focused and open-ended questions are better than one hundred yes or no questions. Construct your questions to allow the seller to tell his story. It is much like being a talk show host; you want them to be comfortable and open up with you. The best way to do this is with positive and nonconfrontational questions, and with follow-up questions.

Some Questions to Ask the Seller

1. Tell me about your business. This is intentionally a very general question While many other buyers have likely asked it, most sellers like talking about their business and are happy to tell you their story.

2. Why has your business been successful?

3. Tell me about your competitors.

4. Are there any key customers that are over, say, 20 percent of your business? If so, tell me about them.

5. What opportunities are there to grow the business? If you were me, just buying the business, what would you do to grow it?

6. What do you do in the business? It is very important for you to know what the seller does and how dependent the business is on him.

7. Tell me about your staff and key employees.

8. What is the impact of you leaving after you sell the business (on employees, customers, suppliers, etc.)? This is actually a follow-up question to "What do you do in the business?" and will give you an idea of how critical to the business the seller is and what the transition will be like. You also want to find out how the seller leaving will impact any key customers.

9. Is the business seasonal? (Omit this question if you already know the answer.)

10. Financials: If the business is represented by a professional business broker, you likely will have summarized financial statements as part of the business profile. For example, VR intermediaries recast the financial statements and include these in the business profile that you receive after signing a confidentiality agreement (or nondisclosure agreement). If there are things you do not understand in the business profile or financials, ask the broker before you visit; if he does not know the answer, he can let the sellers know in advance so they are prepared. Many sellers do not prepare their own financial statements, and they frequently cannot answer questions about them off the top of their heads.

11. Why are you selling your business? Every buyer asks this question, and you need to ask it again because you need to hear it from the sellers. Save this question for last.

Questions Not to Ask

1. Why should I buy this business? This comes off as a trick question at best, or arrogant at worst. It usually annoys sellers, and frankly they have no idea why you should buy this business. It is up to you to figure out if it works for you; they already know it works for them. The sellers have no idea what your capabilities are and what you want.

2. Would you accept X number of dollars? Never start negotiating in your first meeting, and never discuss price in your first meeting. In fact, never discuss price or terms before you have made an offer. There is absolutely nothing to discuss; you have not even made an offer yet. If you are burning with curiosity, you can ask the broker privately; however, the broker probably will not disclose anything because the broker cannot disclose what the seller would accept, even if he or she knows. Make your offer first, and then move on to negotiations and counteroffers.

3. Will you carry a note? Same as above, this is not the time to start negotiating. You can ask the broker privately. Make your offer and go from there.

4. Can I talk to your employees? This will make a seller very nervous and rightly so. All sellers are very concerned about confidentiality, and they are especially concerned about their employees finding out the business is for sale, as they may become concerned and leave. The employees are never told about the sale until after an offer has been made and accepted, and often they are not told until after escrow is opened or even until closing. Notifying the employees is covered in the transition plan in chapter 19, "My 100-Day Plan."

5. Can I talk to your customers? Again, sellers are very concerned about confidentiality. They worry that if their customers find out the business is for sale, they may become concerned about the long-term stability of the business and take their business elsewhere. After you have bought the business, going to customers along with the previous owner to explain you have recently bought the business or are buying it is a different matter. As the new owner, you can introduce yourself and reassure them you will continue to be a good supplier.

6. Don't ask questions that imply the information in the business profile or information provided is false. I have seen buyers effectively accuse or imply the seller's information is false or an outright fabrication

(e.g., financial information). If you don't understand it, that's fine; ask them to explain it. If you don't believe it, that's fine too, but keep that opinion to yourself. Tell them you don't understand it, and ask them to explain it. I cannot count the times I have seen buyers flatly state that the financial information cannot be correct, they don't believe it, and to the chagrin of the buyer, have it turn out to be correct. They did not understand how the information was presented or calculated. No matter. After that, the seller was pretty much done with them.

7. Don't start due diligence now. There will be a number of things that are summarized early on, most notably the financial statements. In your early meetings, asking general questions is fine. This is not the time to start drilling down and asking for proof of the gross sales, expenses, or net profit. For now, you have to assume the figures and information the seller is providing is accurate. Your offer will state that the seller represents that all of the information is correct and accurate. Your offer will also state that you will have a due diligence period as part of your contingencies. It is during this period that you will have the opportunity to verify the seller's claims and review the books and records to your satisfaction. Due diligence is when you roll up your sleeves and dig into the details. For now, understand what is presented, and assume the figures are correct until your offer is accepted and you start due diligence. One caveat on this: if the figures are completely unbelievable and make no sense, this is a different matter. If the seller cannot reasonably explain the summarized figures, then it may be time to walk away.

Some Guidelines

1. Upon arrival, let the sellers know that you respect their time and appreciate them meeting with you, and that you intend to keep the meeting to roughly an hour. I have seen many buyer–seller meetings go on for two hours or even longer. Ironically, most of the buyer's questions were answered in the first hour or ninety minutes; after that, it typically becomes chit chat and more of the same questions.

2. Don't ask the same question twice, and don't ask it again a different way. Pay attention. If he already answered this previously as part of another question, move on.

3. If you don't understand the answer to a question, let them know and ask the sellers to explain it. Don't move on and ask it again later.

4. Don't read from a script. It is tempting to make a list. The problem is, most people tend to read from the list, which makes the meeting very impersonal. I have seen people read the list in its entirety, asking many questions that were answered previously. It becomes exhausting. Notes are fine; a comprehensive list that is read from line by line like a script pretty much kills the meeting.

5. Be efficient in your questions. Focus on important questions and issues. Skip the small stuff, and don't get sidetracked on chit chat. Stay on topic.

6. Do your homework before the meeting. Read and learn what you can before the meeting so you don't have to waste time asking basic questions. Get what you can from the broker, the business profile, and other resources, so when you meet you are sharp, well-informed, and ready to talk intelligently about the business. Some small businesses will have little information available before the meeting; this is fine, do the best you can and get what you can from the broker before the meeting.

Seller Red Flags

1. Unmotivated or undermotivated sellers: Unmotivated and undermotivated sellers almost never close the deal, and you are wasting your time if you are dealing with such a seller. Smart brokers will not even list these businesses, but sometimes even the brokers get surprised and get stuck with a seller that is just not all that motivated to sell. Unmotivated and undermotivated sellers want to sell their business, but only if the deal is exactly the way they want it. If you suspect you are dealing with unmotivated sellers, ask them point blank if they are serious about selling. Ask them why they are selling, what they plan to do after they sell, and what their timeline is. If you are stuck on a point in negotiations or in the deal, ask them directly if the sticking point is a deal breaker.

2. Stubborn sellers: Some sellers are motivated to sell their business, and ironically get in their own way because they are stubborn and want to do things their way. You will have to determine whether the sellers are being stubborn or are simply unmotivated. Although the outward appearances are the same, you may be able to work with stubborn sellers if they are sincerely motivated. However, if the sellers are unmotivated, it is almost impossible to close the deal unless you are willing to acquiesce and do it their way, which can be a painful and expensive experience.

3. Untruthful sellers: If the sellers are being untruthful, this is a huge red flag. Where does it stop, and when can you trust them? Misunderstandings happen during a transaction and sometimes appear to be something sinister. If there is a misunderstanding, deal with it directly. If you can patch it up fine, but if the seller appears to be untruthful and untrustworthy, it is time to walk away.

4. Sellers unwilling to provide information, especially during due diligence: If the sellers are not willing to allow you to exam all of their books and records, this is a big red flag and pretty much a deal killer. There is a difference between sellers refusing to allow you to review information and the sellers simply not having information. I discuss this further in chapter 16, "Due Diligence: Show Me the Money." If the sellers do not have the information, you will need to work around this if possible. If they have the information and refuse to allow you to review it, then you may have to walk away.

5. Moving targets: Sellers that keep changing the deal, or keep heaping things on, are a major concern. This does not necessarily mean the sellers are dishonest; it is more likely that they just keep thinking of things they want and aren't capable of finalizing anything. This is a red flag, because people like this can literally keep changing the terms right up to the closing, which can be a big problem for you. If you see this starting to happen, make sure you confirm that this is the final agreement. Put everything in writing, and make sure the sellers sign it. This is another example where it is handy to have a professional intermediary involved; documenting the deal is a key part of an intermediary's job.

Working Through the Deal with the Seller

It is absolutely critical to have the full cooperation of the sellers from the first meeting all the way through to the end of training. In the beginning, you need information from them about the business, and need them to be open with you and share information freely. During negotiations it is much easier to negotiate with someone that likes you and trusts you. It is nearly impossible to get concessions and negotiate with someone that does not trust you. During training, the sellers will be better trainers and teachers if they are working side by side with someone they have grown to like. As you can see, relationships play a critical role in buying and selling a business. I am not saying that every buyer and seller have always liked each other and got along great. In fact, I have seen many transactions where the buyer and seller would barely speak to each other, and somehow the transaction still closed. In all of those cases, it was difficult and stressful on everyone. If you can maintain a professional and courteous relationship all the way through, your transaction will go much better.

I am not implying that you should always give in to the sellers' demands and give up on yours. The deal has to work for you and be right for you. What I am talking about is how you approach and work with the sellers. If the sellers are represented by a broker, you can use the broker as an intermediary to handle any issues that come up, and issues *will* come up. It is the broker's job to handle these issues. Let the broker know what the issue is, and have him or her act as the middleman to resolve it. This way you maintain your relationship with the sellers, by not having to wrestle with them directly over these things. As an example, VR intermediaries are trained in negotiation and conflict resolution. VR professionals likely have successfully dealt with similar situations many times, and can coach you and the sellers on how to resolve them. In fact, if the sellers are represented by a professional broker like a VR intermediary, they have likely been coached as to what to expect and how the transaction will go.

If you are dealing directly with the sellers (e.g., a "For Sale By Owner," or FSBO), you have no choice but to deal directly with the sellers. Working with FSBOs can be very difficult, as neither party has likely ever bought or sold a business. No one really knows how to proceed, and both are pretty much ad-libbing and making it up as they go along. If you are dealing with a FSBO transaction, make sure you stick to the steps in this book, and don't get talked into doing an informal or "under the table" deal. With FSBOs, it is especially important to do a thorough due diligence and valuation estimate (Where did the sellers come up with the price? Did they calculate what the earnings are? Are their figures correct?). You may be thinking, why not get a professional intermediary to represent me on this great FSBO I found? Good idea on the surface, but there is one minor problem. It is a FSBO because the sellers don't want to pay the broker's commission, or maybe they didn't like what the broker told them as far as value goes, so they are doing it on their own. The likelihood of a broker being able to help you with a FSBO is nearly zero, and the big problem is going to be, who is going to pay the commission. Some intermediaries will work as a "buyer's agent" for a fee. This is actually pretty rare, but there are a few that will do it.

In your search for the right business, you will meet a variety of sellers. Some will be friendly and cooperative, others quiet and reserved, and still others almost impossible to get information from or work with. Be patient, courteous, and professional. It will pay you dividends in the end. Most importantly, be prepared to walk away and move on if you must. And by the way, sometimes deals die only to come back to life again, so keep an open mind even if you do need to walk away.

Let's take a look at a success story of a business that sold, and two examples of businesses that did not sell.

Buyer asks the Right Questions and Buys Distribution Company

Sam owned a specialty industrial distribution company and loved his business, but it was time to retire. His business had great earnings, had been operating for over twenty-five years, and had been run very well. Sam had a parade of prospective buyers. All were interested in the business because it had excellent earnings, but few were capable of running it, and few saw the true value of the company (in fact, a few said it was way over priced). As this parade of buyers passed through, Sam grew frustrated with the redundant questions, and even more frustrated with those that started questioning the value of the business before they even understood the business.

Finally Rick appeared. Rick was a buyer that really understood the business and not only saw the intrinsic value the business presently had, but also what the business could be. Sam and Rick immediately connected, and Rick ultimately bought the business.

It was interesting to watch prospective buyers spend hours asking irrelevant, minor questions and leave the seller meeting knowing nothing about the business. They wasted their time and the seller's, as they didn't do their homework before they met with him and consequently didn't even know what questions to ask. Many of these meetings were like a bad blind date—there was not much communication, and the relationship never went beyond the first meeting. Only Rick saw the big picture. The point here is that a lot of buyers missed this opportunity because they did not build a relationship with the seller, did not take the time to learn about the business, wasted time asking generic questions, missed the big picture, and consequently passed on a great business without even realizing it.

Another important point here is the relationship Rick built with Sam. Rick was genuinely interested in the business, did his homework, and started building a relationship with Sam from the first meeting. Consequently it was much easier for Rick to negotiate with Sam as Sam really wanted Rick to buy the business because he liked him and trusted him. And when Rick needed help or advice Sam was always ready and willing to be there to help out. In fact, after taking a few months off, Sam actually went to work for Rick part-time to keep busy and to see his customers who had become buddies over the past twenty-five years.

Seller's Remorse Strikes, Seller Turns Down Offers and Never Sells

Edward has a very successful manufacturing company and the earnings are excellent. It has a unique product line, with limited competition. The business was worth $1.6 million dollars and was initially listed for this. Seller's remorse struck early, and Edward decided to raise the price. That's right. He increased his asking price while the business was on the market and just a few weeks into it. What was the basis for his price increase? He felt $1.6 million was not enough money to meet his retirement needs; he did some calculations on his own, decided he needed more, and by his calculations it was worth more. So the price was increased. What is fascinating is what happened. An offer came in for $2 million dollars, more than the original asking price and the calculated market value, and he turned it down. Edward didn't like the terms, as there was a sizable seller note in addition to the SBA financing, and he wasn't comfortable with the buyer. Another offer was made by a competitor, this one for $2.4 million. The price was a premium, but the offer was a very creative one, with 100 percent financing consisting of a large bank loan and again a seller note to make up the difference. Again, Edward turned down the offer. In the end Edward, did not sell his business; he opted to have a family member take over while he stayed on part-time.

This is an excellent example of an unmotivated seller or, at best, an undermotivated seller. Although Edward wanted to sell his business and retire, his first priority was to fetch a premium for the business on his terms, and money was his primary motivation. As buyers showed interest and offers came in, his expectations of what he could get increased steadily. The negotiations were a classic example of win–lose negotiations. Sellers that are motivated strictly by financial gain are nearly impossible to work with, as the deal will never be good enough, and they will always want just a little more.

Great Business, Lousy Books & Records

Tom owns a construction company. It is a great business, has excellent earnings, and has a specialty where the competition is somewhat limited. His business was on the market for two years and never sold. Tom was a great seller to work with; he was very cooperative, a nice guy, and was actually willing to be flexible in the sale.

So why didn't his business sell? While Tom's business was actually a good-sized one, with sales over $2 million a year, his books and records were terrible. A few buyers were interested in the business and wanted to make an offer, but they had problems confirming the earnings. In the end, the buyers and the bank could not get past the books and records, and Tom's business never sold.

The buyers were right to walk away from the business. Although I am confident the earnings were real, the books and records were such that even if the buyer accepted the claimed earnings, the bank would not approve a loan, and the buyer could not get financing. In the end there was not a deal to be had, at least not until the books and records are cleaned up and the earnings are provable.

Chapter 10: It's All about EARNINGS!

Alphabet soup—what do these mean: DE, SDE, SDC, EBITDA, EBIT, and pretax profit?

With the exception of pretax profit, of course, all of the above are acronyms for earnings (defined on the following page). Each is a different earnings figure, a different measure of profitability. Is there one that is best? That depends upon what you are looking for. Wall Street uses EBITDA, business brokers use DE (also known as SDE, and formerly as SDC, or SDCF), and the IRS uses pretax profit (net profit) from your tax return to determine your taxable income. For any given business, each of these figures is very different. In fact, an owner wants to maximize his DE, as this is his paycheck so to speak, and minimize his pretax profit to reduce his taxable income. So you can imagine how different these figures are. It may seem crazy that one profit figure could be increased while another is minimized, but in fact this is how every business is run, even big businesses. The goal is to maximize cash flow and minimize taxes. Based on this, the net profit, or pretax profit, on a company's tax return is not a good measure of what the business is really earning, as the accountants are busily working away minimizing the company's taxes, which means minimizing the net profit. Let's face it: no one wants to pay extra taxes. So which earnings figure do we use when we are looking at a prospective business? As an owner or buyer, the earnings figure you are primarily concerned with is DE, as this is the owner's total economic benefit from owning the business (see below) and is used for valuing small and midsize businesses. So for a buyer, it is important to understand what DE is and how to calculate it.

When you are searching for businesses, the DE will be stated in the advertisement and in the business profile. Some may call it "cash flow," which it is not; others may call it earnings; and yet others may call it SDE or SDC. It is all the same, and it is all calculated the same way. When you are sifting through the ads on the Internet and reviewing business profiles, you will not have enough information to calculate the DE on your own; so at that stage you just have to go with the stated figure and understand that you will have an opportunity to verify the figures during due diligence. Although you will not have sufficient information to verify the DE during the search stage, it is still important to know how it is calculated so you can understand the figures on the business profiles for the businesses you are reviewing. During due diligence, it is vital that you understand how a P&L is recast to arrive at the DE for the business, as well as how "add backs" are handled. Even if you decide to use your CPA to review the financials, you should still have a good understanding of this since you are the one buying the business and making the final decision.

Before we learn how to calculate DE, let's take a closer look at the definitions of each type of earnings.

Earnings Definitions

DE – Discretionary earnings; also called SDE, and formerly called SDC: DE is the owner's total economic benefit from operating and owning the business. DE is calculated by taking the net profit from the business tax returns and adding back all of the owner's benefits, such as owners salary, health insurance/life insurance, auto expenses (personal only), and other owner's benefits, plus interest, taxes, depreciation, and amortization (just like EBITDA below, plus the owner's benefits). SDE (seller's discretionary earnings) and SDC (seller's discretionary cash) are also terms used for DE. The calculation and earnings figure is the same.

EBITDA – Earnings before interest, taxes, depreciation, and amortization: EBITDA is typically used as an earnings figure for very large companies. It is much like DE, except owner's benefits are not added back. For larger companies, the management salaries, including the salary of the chief executive officer (CEO), are included in this figure. So this figure is basically the earnings of a professionally run or absentee-run company.

EBIT – Earnings before interest and taxes: EBIT is similar to EBITDA, except depreciation and amortization are not added back. EBIT is not commonly used; EBITDA is the preferred figure.

Pretax profit or net profit: This is the figure from the business's P&L statement and tax returns. For a large company, management salaries will be included in this figure. For small businesses, owners' salaries may or may not be included in this figure, depending on how they take their compensation. Never make assumptions on what is and is not included in the P&L of a small business. Always confirm these details during due diligence, as it can drastically change the profit figure. This figure is not a meaningful representation of the company's true earnings because the owner's CPA has worked hard to minimize the reported profit in order to reduce taxes.

What's the difference between DE and EBITDA? They seem similar. DE and EBITDA are similar and yet are importantly different. DE includes all of the owner's benefits from owning the business, so it is the owner's total earnings from the business, with zero debt (remember interest was added back). EBITDA includes the salaries of the professional managers running the business; for example, the CEO and chairman. If a company is a publicly held company (traded on a stock exchange), there isn't an "owner" running it, so DE is meaningless, and EBITDA is a better figure for earnings. For a small or midsize company, DE more accurately reflects the total economic benefit of owning the business.

DE is calculated by taking the net profit from the company's tax return and, first, adding back interest, depreciation, and amortization (if any). At this point you now have the company's EBITDA. That was the easy part, and now the real work starts. Next you add back the owner's personal benefits (also known as "perks") from the business, including the owner's salary, and any "nonoperational" expenses. This is where calculating the DE gets interesting. Many add-backs are straightforward, easily documented, and verifiable. Some fall into gray areas regarding their legitimacy or verifiability. So let's talk about add-backs first, and then dive into a couple of examples.

Why are interest, depreciation, and amortization added back in DE and EBITDA? Aren't these expenses? Depreciation and amortization are expenses shown on the tax return; however, they are called "noncash expenses," used to recapture previous investments. If you were to look through the company's check register, you would not find any checks written to depreciation or amortization. There was no cash spent on either of these items. These expenses represent previous major investments, such as equipment, that are being recaptured over a period of time.

For example, if a machine shop bought a piece of equipment for $20,000 four years ago, the cash was spent that year; however, the expense is recaptured over several years, depending on the life of the equipment and IRS rules. It will be shown as depreciation on the current tax returns. This serves as a tax deduction for several years, as the owner is allowed to recapture the expense over time; however, as you can see, it is not an actual cash expense for that particular year. This is why depreciation is called a noncash expense and is added back in calculating the DE or EBITDA for a business.

Why is interest added back? Interest is a cash expense? Interest is added back to get the earnings to a debt-free basis. This is done because whatever the current owner's debt service is, yours will be different. By adding the current owner's interest back, you can use DE as your debt-free earnings, and then subtract your projected debt service to estimate your earnings after debt service (a very important figure). We will discuss earnings after debt service and determining whether the deal pencils out for you in chapter 12, "Does This Deal Work for Me?"

I previously mentioned adding back owner's benefits. Business brokers and lenders commonly refer to these expenses as "add-backs." Owner's benefits, such as salary, health insurance, and personal car expenses, are legitimate add-backs. Expenses required to operate the business are not a legitimate add-back. For example, an owner's trip to Hawaii would be a legitimate add-back if it was not business-related or essential to the operations, while an owner's trip to Las Vegas for a trade show is not a valid add-back since it is part of the business sales and marketing expense and would likely continue with you as an owner. When reviewing add-backs, the determining factor is whether or not they are essential to the business. If the expense is required to operate the business and is business-related, it is not a valid add-back and should be left in the company's expenses. Another very important aspect of add-backs is that the expense being added back must have a corresponding (matching) expense line item on the P&L and tax return, and the owner must be able to show that this amount was actually expensed to the business. Many owners will take an arbitrary figure for some expense categories and claim it as an add-back. It is their job to provide proof during due diligence that these expenses were actually run through the business. Remember that if the add-backs are inflated, the DE will be overstated. Every dollar of add-backs is a dollar added to the DE, which inflates the value of the business.

When initially looking at businesses, it is overwhelmingly tempting for some to dig into the details and start going through the P&L line by line, questioning every expense and add-back. A word of caution on this: during your initial review of the business, focus on the big picture, and don't get into the details just yet. You will have time for that later. Start with the basic questions and the big picture, make note of detailed questions you have for later, and don't get bogged down in details. First find out if you even like the business, and if it is a prospect, then you can move on to the details. In fact, in the early stages you won't have a copy of the P&Ls or tax returns anyway. That comes later, after you have made an offer. If you start asking for verification of the financials or the add-backs and DE before you know anything about the business, the broker and seller will simply write you off as a novice or a shopper and stop working with you. It is too early to dig into details. You first need to look at the business and decide whether you are even interested. Verifying the DE and add-backs is done during due diligence, after you have looked at the business and made an offer. For now, accept the stated figures, and make a note of things that are questionable or that you don't understand; you will have your opportunity to verify them during due diligence. It is appropriate, however, to ask general questions about the DE and how it was arrived at so you can understand it. Just don't cross the line and attempt to verify each line item.

You are going to go through the recasting several times. Your first pass is when you are considering making an offer on the business. In working up the first pass of the recasting, it is best to go with the stated add-backs to verify that the recasting was done correctly. Often buyers are tempted to immediately point out what they believe to be discrepancies in the add-backs or recasting and to argue over what the DE really is; however, many times the perceived mistakes are not errors; they are just poorly explained add-backs or perhaps a poorly documented recasting. If there are errors in the recasting or add-backs that are questionable or inappropriate, note them and ask for clarification if you decide to make an offer. With your first-pass recasting complete, you can work up a value estimate, calculate your offer price, and determine whether the deal pencils out for you or not. Working up a value estimate is discussed in chapter 11, "What's It Worth to Me?" Determining whether the deal pencils out for you is discussed in chapter 12, "Does This Deal Work for Me?"

When you are doing your first pass of the recasting, you probably won't have a copy of the P&Ls or tax returns, as these are not typically given to a buyer until an offer is made and has been accepted. So on your first pass, you will be using the figures from the business profile or whatever the broker or owner has made available. For now this is OK. You are just using these figures to confirm that the DE was calculated correctly (basically checking the math), and then using the recast worksheet to work up a value estimate in case you want to make an offer.

After your offer has been accepted, the work starts. You now are going to go through the recasting in detail, verifying each add-back, as well as verifying the figures in the financial statements. Verifying the DE is part of due diligence, which is covered in detail in chapter 16, "Due Diligence: Show Me the Money!" You may find add-backs in due diligence that are either overstated or are not legitimate. If this occurs, you can revise your offer to reflect the actual DE for the business.

Note: A good explanation of financial statements and depreciation is in *How to Read a Financial Report: Wringing Vital Signs Out of the Numbers*[7] or *Reading Financial Reports for Dummies*.[1] If you need a further explanation, see your CPA. If you do not understand the financial information for a business you are looking at, have your CPA review it and explain it to you.

Calculating Discretionary Earnings

We will go through two examples of calculating the DE for two different businesses, Acme Industrial Distributors and Way High Manufacturing. Both examples are hypothetical, and the figures are fictitious, but in line with typical businesses of their size. Both recast P&Ls were done on the earnings and value spreadsheet available at *www.mybusinessbroker.com,* where these examples are also available for you to print out for reference. The earnings and value spreadsheet also includes graphs (see below) showing sales and DE over the past three years.

You will see a variety of formats for summarized financial statements in business profiles. The examples below are fairly comprehensive recast P&Ls. Some business brokers will provide you with business profiles containing a complete recast P&L like these; others will provide a summarized version with minimal detail. During the search stage, the summarized version is sufficient to determine whether the business is of interest to you or not, and even sufficient to write an offer, as you will have the opportunity to verify everything during due diligence. Of course, if the figures make no sense or are completely unbelievable, then you should move on if the broker is unable or unwilling to explain this, at least at a summary level.

Acme Industrial Distributors Example

Below is the recast P&L example for Acme Industrial Distributors using the earnings-value worksheet available at *www.mybusinessbroker.com*. You can print a full-size copy of the Acme Industrial Distributors example from my Web site at *www.mybusinessbroker.com*.

Acme Industrial Distributors				
Revenue	**3 Years Ago**	**2 Years Ago**	**Last Year**	**Notes**
Gross Sales	$760,000	$800,000	$835,000	
Other Income				
Total Revenue	**$760,000**	**$800,000**	**$835,000**	
Cost of Goods Sold	**$410,000**	**$430,000**	**$450,000**	
Gross Profit	**$350,000**	**$370,000**	**$385,000**	
Gross Margin %	46%	46%	46%	
Expenses				
Advertising	$3,000	$3,000	$3,000	
Amortization			$0	
Auto	$15,000	$20,000	$20,000	
Bad Debt	$1,000	$1,000	$1,000	
Bank Charges	$1,000	$1,000	$1,000	
Depreciation	$15,000	$15,000	$15,000	
Dues & Subscriptions	$500	$500	$500	
Employee Benefits	$4,000	$4,000	$5,000	
Insurance	$13,000	$15,000	$17,000	
Interest	$5,000	$5,000	$5,000	
Legal & Accounting	$2,500	$3,000	$3,250	
Payroll	$65,000	$70,000	$75,000	
Other Payroll	$0	$0	$0	
Outside Labor	$3,000	$4,000	$5,000	
Owner's Salary	$75,000	$75,000	$75,000	
Payroll Taxes	$7,150	$7,700	$8,250	
Rent	$48,000	$50,000	$50,000	
Repairs & Maintenance	$4,000	$4,000	$5,000	
Supplies	$7,000	$8,000	$10,000	
Telephone	$10,000	$11,000	$12,000	
Travel & Entertainment	$10,000	$10,000	$10,000	
Utilities	$14,000	$14,000	$15,000	
Total Expenses	**$303,150**	**$321,200**	**$336,000**	
Net Profit	**$46,850**	**$48,800**	**$49,000**	
Add Backs (Expense Adjustments)				
Amortization				
Depreciation	$15,000	$15,000	$15,000	
Interest	$5,000	$5,000	$5,000	
Owner's Salary	$75,000	$75,000	$75,000	
Owner's Personal Auto Expense	$8,000	$10,000	$10,000	Owner & Wife cars
Owner's health insurance	$9,000	$9,000	$10,000	family health ins
Travel & Entertainment	$5,000	$6,000	$8,000	personal T&E
Supplies	$2,000	$4,000	$3,000	Personal expenses
Total Add Backs/Adjustments	$119,000	$124,000	$126,000	
Discretionary Earnings (DE)	***$165,850***	***$172,800***	***$175,000***	

Acme Industrial Distributors						
Financial Summary						
	3 Years Ago	2 Years Ago	Last Year	Current Annualized	3 Year Avg	Wtd Avg 10/20/70
Gross Sales	$760,000	$800,000	$835,000	$850,000	$798,333	$820,500
Cost of Goods Sold	$410,000	$430,000	$450,000	$459,000	$430,000	$442,000
Gross Margin $	$350,000	$370,000	$385,000	$391,000	$368,333	$378,500
Gross Margin %	46.1%	46.3%	46.1%	46.0%	46.1%	46.1%
Total Expenses	$303,150	$321,200	$336,000	$337,000	$320,117	$329,755
Net Profit	$46,850	$48,800	$49,000	$54,000	$48,217	$48,745
Expense Adjustments	$119,000	$124,000	$126,000	$126,000	$123,000	$124,900
DE	$165,850	$172,800	$175,000	$180,000	$171,217	$173,645
DE %	21.8%	21.6%	21.0%	21.2%	21.4%	21.2%
Notes:						
1. Weighted Averate is 10% X 3 years ago + 20% X 2 Years ago + 70% X Last Year						
2. 3 Year Average is average of last three complete years.						
3. Current annualized is this year annualized if data is available.						

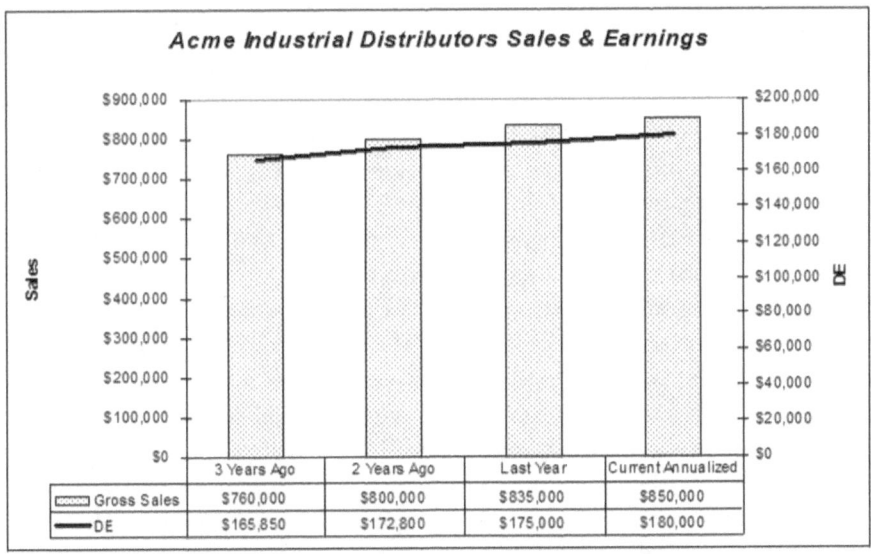

Let's review the recast spreadsheet for Acme Industrial.

The first step in recasting a financial statement is entering the revenue and expense figures from the P&L or tax return. The earnings-value worksheet already has the common expense and income categories, you can edit and change these if need be. When you start due diligence, it is best to use tax returns since they are more reliable; if you use the P&L to obtain more detail on the expenses, make sure you compare the figures with the tax returns. The figures from the financial statement are entered in the top section of the spreadsheet exactly as they appear on the statement; no adjustments are made at this point. You should use the same category descriptions that are on the financial statement so you can compare and check these figures later. Note that the recast spreadsheet has columns for the last three years, and a separate sheet is provided for the year-to-date (not shown above). It is preferable to get figures for the last three years and the year-to-date in order to get a good understanding of how the business has performed historically, what the trends look like, and how it is performing now. The DE for the last full year is used to calculate the value based on the comparable sales multiple, which is discussed in the next chapter.

If the tax return and P&L do not match, you need to pick one to use for your recasting; the tax return is always preferred. If you mix and match figures from both the P&L and tax return and the two documents don't match, your figures will be off, and it will be difficult to reconcile the figures. So pick one and use it as your primary document; the other can be used as a reference if necessary.

Now that the stated figures are entered, you can work on the adjustments (add-backs). Start with amortization, depreciation, and interest. These are always added back and are separate line items on the financial statement. Note that if they do not appear on the financial statement you are recasting from, then they should not be added back. This is where it can get a bit confusing. Many small company P&Ls do not show amortization and depreciation, as these are not actual cash expenses. They often are calculated by the owner's accountant at year end and shown only on the tax returns. If this is the case, the total expenses from the tax return and P&L will not match. The expenses shown on the tax return will be higher by the total amount of the amortization and depreciation, and the net profit shown on the tax return will be lower by this amount. This is a great example of why financial statements are recast. While the net profit on the tax return and P&L are different, the DE for both should be exactly the same. Why? Amortization and depreciation are added back, which will adjust the tax return expenses to be the same as the P&L, resulting in exactly the same DE for both.

The next step in doing the adjustments is to add back the owner's benefits. This can get tricky, because this is the area where owners often get creative as far as what is a personal or a non-operational expense. Inflating the add-backs increases the business's DE dollar for dollar and consequently increases the value of the business. As a result, owners have strong financial motivation to classify as much as possible as an owner benefit to increase the value of their business. In the Acme example above, the add-backs are shown at the bottom of the worksheet. All of the add-backs are totaled, and the sum is then added to the net profit (hence the term add-back, because these expenses are added back) to arrive at the DE.

The add-backs for Acme are typical for a small business: owner's salary, owner's auto expenses, owner's health insurance, travel and entertainment, and supplies. These are typical of the types of expenses you will see added back in a small business. The fact that an add-back looks OK does not mean it is valid. You will confirm the validity of the add-backs during due diligence. During the valuation phase, when you are preparing to make an offer, you are just confirming that the recasting was done correctly, looking for obvious errors, and working up a value estimate.

Entering the data and doing the math for a recasting is actually fairly straightforward. The trick is making sure that the figures are correct and that the add-backs are valid, which comes later.

Way High Manufacturing Example

Let's take a look at another example, below is the recast P&L for Way High Manufacturing, again you can print a full size copy of this example from my website at *www.mybusinessbroker.com.*

Way High Manufacturing				
Income	**3 Years Ago**	**2 Years Ago**	**Last Year**	**Notes**
Gross Sales	$1,188,000	$1,350,000	$1,500,000	
Other Income				
Total Income	**$1,188,000**	**$1,350,000**	**$1,500,000**	
Cost of Goods Sold	**$507,600**	**$564,000**	**$600,000**	
Gross Profit	**$680,400**	**$786,000**	**$900,000**	
Gross Margin %	57%	58%	60%	
Expenses				
Advertising	$4,000	$4,000	$5,000	
Amortization			$0	
Auto	$30,000	$40,000	$40,000	
Bad Debt	$1,000	$1,000	$1,000	
Bank Charges	$1,000	$1,000	$1,000	
Depreciation	$30,000	$30,000	$30,000	
Dues & Subscriptions	$1,000	$1,000	$1,000	
Employee Benefits	$5,000	$8,000	$10,000	
Insurance	$25,000	$27,000	$30,000	
Interest	$10,000	$10,000	$10,000	
Legal & Accounting	$4,000	$4,500	$5,000	
Payroll	$300,000	$360,000	$400,000	
Other Payroll	$0	$0	$0	
Outside Labor	$7,000	$9,000	$10,000	
Owner's Salary	$100,000	$100,000	$100,000	
Payroll Taxes	$33,000	$39,600	$44,000	
Rent	$56,000	$58,000	$60,000	
Repairs & Maintenance	$10,000	$10,000	$10,000	
Supplies	$12,000	$18,000	$20,000	
Telephone	$16,000	$18,000	$20,000	
Travel & Entertainment	$13,000	$16,000	$20,000	
Utilities	$20,000	$23,000	$25,000	
Total Expenses	**$678,000**	**$778,100**	**$842,000**	
Net Profit	**$2,400**	**$7,900**	**$58,000**	
Add Backs (Expense Adjustments)				
Amortization				
Depreciation	$30,000	$30,000	$30,000	
Interest	$10,000	$10,000	$10,000	
Owner's Salary	$100,000	$100,000	$100,000	
Owner's Personal Auto Expense	$15,000	$20,000	$20,000	Owner & Wife cars
Owner's health insurance	$10,000	$11,000	$12,000	family health ins
Travel & Entertainment	$8,000	$10,000	$15,000	personal T&E
Supplies	$2,000	$4,000	$5,000	Personal expenses
Total Add Backs/Adjustments	$175,000	$185,000	$192,000	
Discretionary Earnings (DE)	$177,400	$192,900	$250,000	

Way High Manufacturing Financial Summary						
	3 Years Ago	2 Years Ago	Last Year	Current Annualized	3 Year Avg	Wtd Avg 10/20/70
Gross Sales	$1,188,000	$1,350,000	$1,500,000	$1,575,000	$1,346,000	$1,438,800
Cost of Goods Sold	$507,600	$564,000	$600,000	$630,000	$557,200	$583,560
Gross Margin $	$680,400	$786,000	$900,000	$945,000	$788,800	$855,240
Gross Margin %	57.3%	58.2%	60.0%	60.0%	58.5%	59.4%
Total Expenses	$678,000	$778,100	$842,000	$882,700	$766,033	$812,820
Net Profit	$2,400	$7,900	$58,000	$62,300	$22,767	$42,420
Expense Adjustments	$175,000	$185,000	$192,000	$192,000	$184,000	$188,900
DE	$177,400	$192,900	$250,000	$254,300	$206,767	$231,320
DE %	14.9%	14.3%	16.7%	16.1%	15.4%	16.1%
Notes:						
1. Weighted Averate is 10% X 3 years ago + 20% X 2 Years ago + 70% X Last Year						
2. 3 Year Average is average of last three complete years.						
3. Current annualized is this year annualized if data is available.						

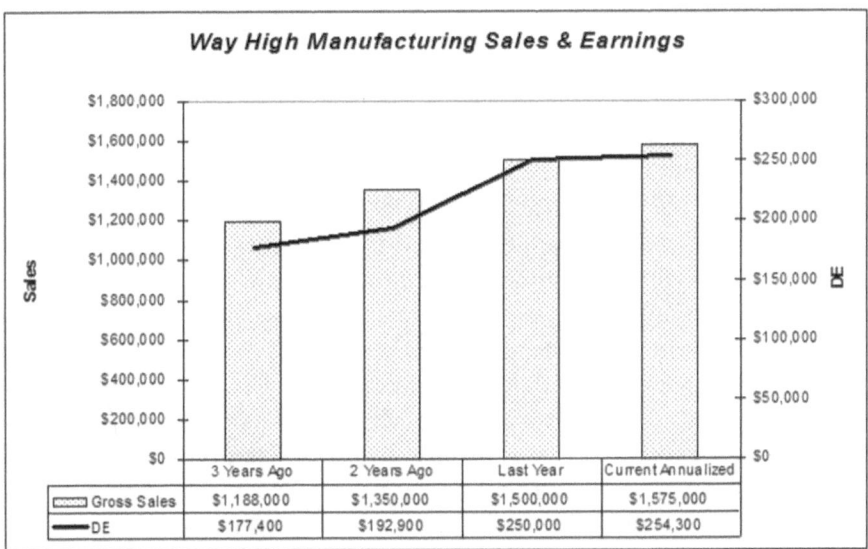

Way High Manufacturing Sales & Earnings

	3 Years Ago	2 Years Ago	Last Year	Current Annualized
Gross Sales	$1,188,000	$1,350,000	$1,500,000	$1,575,000
DE	$177,400	$192,900	$250,000	$254,300

Let's go through the recasting and add-backs for Way High Manufacturing. The process is the same regardless of the type or size of company. While the process is the same, there are some interesting differences between Acme and Way High.

Again, the first step is to enter the revenue and expense figures from the P&L or tax return, and then enter the add-backs. You will notice that the add-backs for Way High are higher than those for Acme. The owner's salary is higher; likewise the owner's benefits (auto expenses, travel and entertainment, and insurance) are higher as well. This is typical; companies with higher earnings and cash flow usually have higher add-backs. Owners and their accountants will increase the owners' benefits and expenses in order to minimize the taxes for the company. So a large amount of add-backs for the owners' benefits is not necessarily a red flag, although it does need to be verified during due diligence.

Some other interesting differences between Acme and Way High are the fact that Acme has a very steady history, with consistent growth, conservative add-backs, and a consistent bottom line. This is always comforting to a prospective buyer. Way High has had strong growth in both sales and DE over the past three years, which makes the business attractive, as it is growing. At the same time, this may cause a prospective buyer to question the figures. High growth in sales and earnings is not necessarily a red flag; it just needs to be explained when you meet with the seller and confirmed during due diligence.

Another aspect of Way High that often troubles buyers is that the net profit was very low in prior years, and even in the current year is fairly low in comparison to the DE. Buyers often look at the tax return net profit and somehow try to connect that to the DE or actual profit of the company. The net profit of a company shown on the tax returns has very little relationship to the real earnings of the company, the DE. The best way to think of the net profit shown on the tax returns is to consider it as one element of the DE, or your first step to calculating the DE, and to remember that you cannot use this figure to judge the earnings of the company. The net profit on the tax returns is a tax figure; it is not an accurate reflection of the actual earnings of the company. For example, consider the fact that Acme has a higher net profit historically and a similar net profit last year, but less add-backs than Way High, resulting in a lower DE than Way High. As you can see, a higher net profit does not necessarily mean higher DE. In fact, the net profit alone doesn't mean much at all. It is just a figure on the tax returns, which is why recasting is so important. Which business would you pay more for?

The P&Ls used for Acme and Way High were intentionally kept simple so we could focus on the steps involved in recasting a financial statement. Actual P&Ls and add-backs will vary widely for each business you look at. Some may be well documented and easy to follow, and many will have add-backs in a variety of expense categories. In your initial recasting, you will use the stated figures; during due diligence you will verify not only the amount of each add-back, but also the validity. The next obvious question is, "what about a business with poor books or a cash business? How do I calculate the DE for a business like that?"

Many small businesses, such as restaurants, retail businesses, small service businesses, and even small wholesale businesses, have very limited financial statements. It is often very difficult to recast the P&L and determine the DE for these businesses. The best way to handle this type of business is to focus on the gross sales, and calculate what your operating expenses would likely be. You can enter the gross sales on the recast spreadsheet, and then enter your estimates for the operating expenses using what information you have available from the seller. This will give you an estimate of what the DE should be for this business. The fact that DE is very difficult to calculate is why brokers often value these businesses using the gross sales. You should treat any DE figure you come up with for a business as an estimate, and it is wise to be conservative in your figures, using a range of expenses to come up with a best-case and worst-case estimate. While you must be careful in estimating what the real earnings of these businesses are, and the financial records may make it difficult to verify the actual earnings, there are many very good small businesses on the market. If you find a good one, it may be worth the extra work.

What about cash businesses? Many small businesses have a significant amount of cash going through the business, and some of these owners underreport the sales of the business on their tax return. They can certainly spin a compelling story as to why they hide some of their income to save on taxes, and it may sound believable. The problem is what do you believe and what figure do you use? If they cannot absolutely prove their claimed cash sales and additional earnings, you should not take their word for it, and certainly should not pay for it. The basic rule with respect to unreported sales and earnings is that if they can't prove it, it didn't happen, and you shouldn't pay for it.

Now that you know how to calculate the DE for a business, let's take a look at how to estimate the value.

Chapter 11: What's It Worth to Me?

Perhaps one of the most challenging aspects of buying a business is determining how much it is worth. No one wants to overpay for anything, especially for something as expensive and important as a business. The problem is, how do you determine what the value is? This question plagues and frustrates many buyers, and sellers too for that matter. Business valuation is a complex topic; obviously business valuation cannot be covered in one chapter, so we will take a different approach. We will explore some methods to determine whether the price of the business is reasonable—a sanity check, if you will, that you can use to see whether the price is sensible or not, and to guide you as to what you may want to offer for a business. You won't want to go through the exercise of calculating the value of every business you look at. Even with the simple methods we will learn here, it does take time. When you are interested in a business and are considering it as a serious prospect, that is the point where you sit down and spend some time determining the market value and your value for the business. By the way, just because you spent some time gathering data and comparable sales figures, don't expect the seller, or the broker for that matter, to necessarily agree with you on your estimate of the market value. You will have your data and your opinion, and the sellers will have theirs; it is unlikely they will be the same. The value of a business is the most hotly debated issue between buyer and seller. Resolving this difference of opinion happens after an offer is made and negotiations start. If everyone could agree on an exact value, there would be little need to negotiate.

Before we talk about calculating a value, let's discuss a few common value terms, what they mean, and how they are used.

Definitions of Value

> Fair market value: Per IRS Revenue Ruling 59-60, "The price at which the property would change hands between a willing buyer and a willing seller when the former is not under any compulsion to buy and the latter is not under any compulsion to sell, both parties having reasonable knowledge of relevant facts."[6] As a buyer, fair market value

is actually the only value you are concerned with, and while it sounds simple enough, it is actually difficult to calculate an exact value and can be very subjective.

Book value: This is strictly an accounting value for balance sheet purposes and has no relation to the market value of the company or its assets. Book value is the total net assets (depreciated assets) less the total liabilities on the balance sheet. This is an accounting and tax value and sheds no light on the market value of the business or its assets. Some buyers see the book value on the balance sheet and fall into the trap of trying to somehow equate or relate it to the market value of the company. There is absolutely no relationship between the book value of a business and the market value. This figure is useless to you as a prospective buyer; it is only interesting to the IRS and the CPA for tax purposes. That's it.

Asset value: This value is an attempt to arrive at the market value for the tangible assets (inventory, equipment, furniture, etc.). It is basically the book value stepped up to the estimated market value of the assets. It typically does not take into account the intangible assets of the company, although if this has been calculated by an analyst, it may include this.

Liquidation value: This is the value resulting from the sale (liquidation) of the assets (e.g., inventory, equipment, furniture, etc.). The value of the tangible (hard) assets is typically discounted to reflect a forced sale; this value does not include the value of the goodwill or intangible assets of the company.

Goodwill: Goodwill is a component of the market value. Simply put, goodwill is the difference between the market value and the value of the tangible assets; or stated another way, it is the premium over and above the value of the tangible assets that a buyer pays for the business. Some confuse the accounting term goodwill (which is a specific value) with the goodwill relating to the value of the businesses reputation and customers. While the accounting term is an attempt to put a value on these and other intangible assets of the business, the two are not directly related. It is true that a business with a stellar reputation will likely have a higher market value and higher goodwill value than one with a poor reputation. Likewise a company with a great reputation, but poor financial performance, would have a much lower market value and consequently very little goodwill from an accounting standpoint. The accounting goodwill figure is driven strictly by the market value of the company, which is largely driven by earnings. We are not going to calculate goodwill, as this is a complex exercise, and in the end few agree on this value, especially buyers and sellers. It is important to understand that goodwill is pretty much a plug number; it fills the gap between the market value and asset value and basically is the economic value of the business as a continuing enterprise. Don't get tangled up in this debate with the seller or broker. It simply is not important to you. We will estimate the value of the business in a manner that does not require a goodwill calculation.

There are many other value definitions; however, none are relevant to the value of small, privately held businesses, and you will not likely run into them in your search for a business.

Business valuation is a complex task requiring professional training and a thorough knowledge of financial statements. To make things more confusing, there are several different values (see above) for a business and a variety of valuation methods that professionals use depending on the type and size of business they are analyzing. So which value do you use and how do you figure out what it is? The only value you need be concerned with is the fair market value and what the business is worth to you. In theory, these numbers should be the same; however, as you will see later, the value to you could be different based on your needs and your assessment of the business. You may be willing to pay a bit more than fair market value if the business is a really good fit for you; likewise, if the business has some challenges and needs some work, maybe your opinion of the value is a bit below what the comparable sales and fair market value indicate. The important thing to remember is that the value of a business is not an absolute figure; there are a range of values that are possible.

There are a number of methods for valuing businesses; some are straightforward and easily used, and others are very complex and require special training to completely understand. What is fascinating about valuation methods is that they are essentially art impersonating science. What I mean by this is that with all of the elaborate calculations, every business valuation model at some point requires a judgment call by the person doing the valuation. These judgment calls are in the form of selecting an appropriate weighting factor, discount rate, capitalization rate, asset values, and even the correct earnings figures. Consequently, very different valuations can result for the same business, depending upon who is doing the calculation, what assumptions are used, and what the purpose of the valuation is (e.g., for a transaction, partnership, trust, or bank loan; all will have different valuation approaches and different values). To acquaint you with some of the most common valuation methods, here is a list with a brief explanation of each.

Common Valuation Methods

Excess earnings or income capitalization method: This is a commonly used method by analysts and business brokers. In this approach, the value of the tangible and intangible assets are calculated separately and then added together. Advantages to this approach are that it does result in a value for the goodwill, and it is relatively straightforward to use. IRS Revenue Ruling 68-609, published in 1968, outlines the use and application of this method.

Discounted cash flow (DCF) method: This method is widely used by M&A professionals on larger transactions, and by business analysts on formal valuations. The DCF method uses a forecast of future earnings to arrive at a present value for the business (like the net present value calculation for cash flow analysis). While this is a very elegant approach to valuation, it has two weaknesses. The first is that the earnings forecast drives the value, and an optimistic or exaggerated forecast can result in a highly inflated value. The second is that this method also requires a discount rate to be established. The use of an artificially low discount rate will also inflate the value. Consequently, this approach is very easy to tweak and can be used to inflate the value of the business. In fact, it has been abused by some unscrupulous valuation firms. Done correctly, however, it is a very good approach to valuation. As a buyer, you must be careful to review the assumptions and figures used in this analysis. The only time you would likely see this approach is if the business you are interested in has had a formal third-party valuation. If you do run across a DCF valuation, make sure the earnings forecast is in line with reasonable, even conservative, expectations, and review how the discount rate was calculated.

Rule of thumb: A rule of thumb is a generally accepted earnings multiple or percentage of gross sales typical for a particular type of business. These are useful for a quick estimate; however, they do not take into account the size of the business or earnings level. The weakness with this approach is that it is a generic one-size-fits-all approach and not very accurate.

Market data approach: Also known as the comparative sales and earnings multiple method. This method is similar to the rule of thumb approach in that it uses a multiple of the DE. However, rather than using a generally accepted rule of thumb, this method uses comparable sales data to calculate an actual average or median DE multiple. As this method uses actual historic transactions, the data can be narrowed to a specific industry and range of earnings to closely match the business being evaluated.

There is a place for the more elaborate and complex valuation methods. They are used by business valuation analysts in valuations for bank loans, litigation, and to establish the value for partnerships and trusts, to name a few examples. In these cases, it is essential to have an unbiased value for the company that was arrived at through accepted valuation methods. Business valuation analysts are trained to use these methods, and while at some point they must employ professional judgment, they do so based on experience and training (which is where it becomes art). It isn't possible to teach the more complex valuation methods in just one chapter; in fact, Dr. Shannon Pratt, a renowned economist coauthored a book nearly 900 pages in length dealing exclusively with business valuation.[5]

What we will do in this chapter is discuss a basic valuation approach that will enable you to determine whether a business for sale is priced reasonably or not. You won't be capable of doing a formal business valuation, but you will be capable of doing a sanity check. If you decide you need a formal business valuation, you can always pay for a third-party valuation, which is basically the business equivalent of an appraisal.

In the previous chapter, "It's All About Earnings," I discussed earnings and the fact that earnings drive business value. Most business valuation methods are driven by earnings, so the first step in coming up with a value for the business is to know the DE and the gross sales. At this point you can't verify the DE figure; this is done during due diligence; so for now you will just use the DE figure on the business profile. If there is an obvious error, you can make an adjustment; but be careful with this because the figure may be correct and just not explained correctly or clearly. It is the seller's responsibility to prove the claimed earnings during due diligence; so for now, use the claimed earnings. Although it is too early to start due diligence, it is a good idea to ask the broker to explain the calculation of the DE for the business and walk you through it. Additionally, you should ask the broker to explain how the value was determined.

The simplest method for you to use is known by several names: some call it a "rule of thumb," others call it the "earnings multiple" method, and some know it by "comps," or comparable sales. All of these are very similar in that a multiplier is applied to the DE to arrive at a value. This sounds simple enough, and it is. But what multiplier or multiple do you use?

There is one significant difference between the rule of thumb method and the comps method. The rule of thumb method includes broad guidelines that are applied across an entire industry, regardless of the size of the business and its earnings or trends. The comps method is based on similar (comparable) transactions and can be narrowed to match the size and type of company you are comparing it to. Many brokers use the rule of thumb method for a quick and easy estimate of the market value for a company. While this method is good for a quick estimate, it is not very accurate, and it does not take into account the specifics of the company you are looking at. A rule of thumb valuation is a one-size-fits-all generic approach, much like saying the average value of a home in the United States is $206,000, or the average cost of gas in the United States is $2.10 per gallon. While these figures are a good gauge of housing and gas costs nationwide, they have no direct bearing on the cost of either in your city or how much you would pay the next time you purchase either.

The comparable sales, or comps, method uses data from similar transactions to arrive at an earnings multiple to use to determine the market value of the company you are considering. With comps you can narrow the list of comparable transactions to closely match the company you are considering. Sometimes with very specialized businesses you must use a very broad SIC (also known as NAICS) code or industry category to get enough transactions to form a good comparison. In large industries, you will be able to narrow your list to closely match the company you are looking at. Comps need not be confined to you local area; in general, the multiples are fairly consistent regardless of location. This is mainly because these values are largely driven by economic factors, such as earnings, return on investment (ROI), and to a degree demand. It is best to use comparable sales from within your state or region; however, if there aren't enough transactions to provide good data, then using nationwide transactions for your comparable sales is fine. It is better to have a larger number of similar transactions than it is to have either dissimilar local transactions or only a few to compare.

One important thing to be aware of is to make sure you are applying the data correctly. Some earnings multiples are based on EBITDA, while others are based on DE. EBITDA multiples are always much higher than DE multiples, even for the same business. This is because the DE includes the owner's salary and benefits, and EBITDA does not. The most common figure for small businesses is a multiple based on DE. EBITDA is typically used on much larger businesses, those with sales over $10 million. Another thing to be careful of in applying the data is to consider whether the multiple includes inventory or not. You may have heard people toss around figures like five times earnings or even higher for the value of a company. These high multiples are typically based on EBITDA, and often include inventory, A/R, and possibly other assets. While DE multiples are much lower, the multiple is applied to a higher earnings figure and this figure generally does not include inventory or A/R; A/R and inventory are added to the calculated value separately.

So where on earth does one find these elusive comps? You won't find them on Zillow.com, Realtor.com, or any of the real estate sites. While these sites have hundreds of thousands of comps for homes, they have zero for businesses. There are several sites that specialize in collecting data and providing comps for business sales (see listing below). Most are require a subscription and are intended for use by full-time, professional business brokers and M&A intermediaries. If your broker subscribes to one of these services, he can provide you with comps and work up a market value based on the data. Ask your broker to provide you with comps for the business, and also ask him to walk you through how the value was determined. While you will work up your own market value, you need to understand the basis of how the broker and seller determined the value, what their assumptions were, what DE they used, and how they calculated the DE.

Comparable Sales/Transaction Databases

1. BizBuySell.com – modest charge for comparable sales analysis report; available to public and professionals; see *www.bizbuysell.com*

2. Bizcomps – primarily used by professionals; requires a subscription; see *www.bizcomps.com* or *www.bvmarketdata.com*

3. Institute of Business Appraisers (IBA) market database – primarily used by professionals; requires a subscription see *www.go-iba.org*

4. Done Deals – primarily used by professionals; requires a subscription; see *www.donedeals.com/sitecomposer2*

5. Pratt's Stats – primarily used by professionals; requires a subscription; see *www.bvmarketdata.com*

6. VR comparable sales database – tens of thousands of comparable sales from past VR transactions. Available only to VR intermediaries.

Let's take a look at how to use the BizBuySell.com comps database and valuation report to estimate the market value of our examples, Acme Industrial Distributors and Way High Manufacturing.

You can go to *www.bizbuysell.com* and run a market value report, which is based on comparable sales in the company's database. While this is called a valuation report, this is not to be confused with a formal valuation done by a certified business analyst. This is a very simple report comparing the business you are considering with their database of similar businesses sold; and while it is very simplistic, it is actually a very good tool if used properly. The comparable sales data on BizBuySell.com does not include inventory or A/R, thus the inventory value would be added to the market value estimate from this report.

The first step is to enter the DE (the company calls it cash flow, which is the incorrect term, but they have used this term for years). In the last chapter I talked about earnings and how earnings drive value. The BizBuySell.com valuation report is a great example, as it uses the average DE multiple for the selected comps to multiply against the DE (cash flow) you input to arrive at a market value. The report also uses a multiple (percentage) of gross sales to estimate a value. This method is only of interest on small retail stores and cash businesses where the earnings are extremely difficult to even estimate. Once you have entered the DE and gross sales, then you select the industry segment for the business you are analyzing. You can drill down and narrow the search geographically. I suggest starting with the entire United States on your first pass. You can also remove businesses that are dissimilar (e.g., much larger, much smaller, sold for an unusually high or low figure, etc.) from the comparative analysis. As you narrow your comparative analysis by tightening your comp criteria, you will home in on the market value of this business.

It is very important to narrow your comps data to a range of businesses similar in size (gross sales) and DE. Businesses with substantially higher earnings will sell for a higher earnings (DE) multiple, and businesses with very low earnings are often discounted. So it is very important to set a range of earnings close to the business you are looking at, as the larger ones will inflate the multiple, and the smaller ones will actually pull the value down. Either way, when dissimilar businesses are in your comps report, you don't really have comparable sales. What you have is just lots of data.

Three comps reports from BizBuySell.com are shown below and are reprinted here with the permission of BizBuySell.com: one for a company in the business services market segment (e.g., B2B services), another for business in the industrial manufacturing market segment, and finally one in the wholesale/distribution market segment. We will use the manufacturing and wholesale/distribution comps to work up estimates for Acme and Way High. I included a comp report from the B2B services segment to illustrate how the figures vary between industries. You will also note in the sample reports below that I used two different DE figures in the three reports to illustrate how higher earnings drive higher multiples.

The sold comparable analysis reports below are courtesy of BizBuySell. com and reprinted with the permission of BizBuySell.com.

SOLD COMPARABLES ANALYSIS
Prepared for: Bill Grunau
Business Category: **Services - Other Business Services**
Location of businesses: **All US States**

GROSS INCOME ANALYSIS

No. of businesses in Gross Income analysis	361
Average Sold-For Price	$304,929
Average Gross Income	$592,814
Average Gross Income Multiplier	.51
Median Gross Income Multiplier	.60
Suggested Sold-For Price using the Gross Income Multiplier ($500,000 **X** .60)	**$300,000**

CASH FLOW ANALYSIS

Refined: With cash flow from $100000 to $200000

No. of businesses in Cash Flow analysis	361
Average Sold-For Price	$304,929
Average Cash Flow	$138,899
Average Cash Flow Multiplier	2.19
Median Cash Flow Multiplier	2.14
Suggested Sold-For Price using the Cash Flow Multiplier ($150,000 **X** 2.14)	**$321,000**

SOLD-FOR/ASKING PRICE ANALYSIS

No. of businesses in Asking/Sold-For Price Analysis	361
Average Asking Price	345,023
Average Sold-For Price	303,408
Sold-For Price as a Percentage of Asking Price	87%

SOLD COMPARABLES ANALYSIS
Prepared for: Bill Grunau
Business Category: **Mfg. - Industrial & Comm. Machinery**
Location of businesses: **All US States**

GROSS INCOME ANALYSIS

No. of businesses in Gross Income analysis	22
Average Sold-For Price	$794,454
Average Gross Income	$1,258,018
Average Gross Income Multiplier	.63
Median Gross Income Multiplier	.72
Suggested Sold-For Price using the Gross Income Multiplier ($1,000,000 **X** .72)	**$720,000**

CASH FLOW ANALYSIS

Refined: With cash flow from $150000 to $350000

No. of businesses in Cash Flow analysis	22
Average Sold-For Price	$794,454
Average Cash Flow	$230,268
Average Cash Flow Multiplier	3.45
Median Cash Flow Multiplier	2.95
Suggested Sold-For Price using the Cash Flow Multiplier ($250,000 **X** 2.95)	**$737,500**

SOLD-FOR/ASKING PRICE ANALYSIS

No. of businesses in Asking/Sold-For Price Analysis	22
Average Asking Price	874,045
Average Sold-For Price	794,454
Sold-For Price as a Percentage of Asking Price	90%

SOLD COMPARABLES ANALYSIS
Prepared for: Bill
Business Category: **Wholesale/Dist. - Nondurable Goods**
Location of businesses: **All US States**

GROSS INCOME ANALYSIS

No. of businesses in Gross Income analysis	93
Average Sold-For Price	$593,463
Average Gross Income	$1,933,549
Average Gross Income Multiplier	.30
Median Gross Income Multiplier	.38
Suggested Sold-For Price using the Gross Income Multiplier ($1,500,000 X .38)	**$570,000**

CASH FLOW ANALYSIS

Refined: With cash flow from $150000 to $350000

No. of businesses in Cash Flow analysis	94
Average Sold-For Price	$587,309
Average Cash Flow	$217,497
Average Cash Flow Multiplier	2.70
Median Cash Flow Multiplier	2.42
Suggested Sold-For Price using the Cash Flow Multiplier ($250,000 X 2.42)	**$605,000**

SOLD-FOR/ASKING PRICE ANALYSIS

No. of businesses in Asking/Sold-For Price Analysis	96
Average Asking Price	601,989
Average Sold-For Price	575,094
Sold-For Price as a Percentage of Asking Price	95%

Let's discuss the business services comps first. The business I was considering in this example has DE of $150,000. In the cash flow analysis section, I refined (narrowed) the range to $100,000 to $200,000. This eliminated businesses with less than $100,000 of DE, which would pull the earnings multiple down, and also eliminated businesses with over $200,000, which would inflate the multiple. The business I am looking at is right in the middle of this range. With these criteria I wound up with 361 similar businesses nationwide in my sold comparables analysis, and a median cash flow (DE) multiplier of 2.14. This report also shows the average cash flow multiplier, which is 2.19. In this case, the two figures are very close, but it begs the question what's the difference? The median figure is often a better figure to use, because in some cases the transactions at the extreme high or low end of the data skew the average. As there are a large number of businesses in this report, I could have narrowed it further by selecting a specific region.

The next comps analysis is for a wholesale/distribution company with cash flow (DE) of $250,000. For this report, I specified a range of $150,000 to $350,000, placing this company in the middle of the specified range, and we wound up with ninety-three comparable transactions nationwide. In this case, if we narrowed the analysis further, we would not have enough comparables for a meaningful comparison. The median cash flow multiplier for this analysis was 2.42, with the average at 2.70 (note the bigger spread between the average and median in this case).

The final comps analysis is for an industrial manufacturing company with cash flow (DE) of $250,000. Again, I specified a range of $150,000 to $350,000, placing this company in the middle of the specified range. This time we wound up with twenty-two comparable transactions nationwide. The median cash flow multiplier was 2.95, and the average cash flow multiplier was 3.45. This is a huge range, and obviously there is a wide range of values in this analysis. The problem is that the analysis only has a sample of twenty-two transactions, so the data is very limited. Although there is a fairly wide range between the average and median, we can still use this data as long as we recognize that our value estimate is just that, an estimate, and that the actual market value is going to have a range of possibilities (e.g., somewhere between 2.95 X DE and 3.45 X DE).

It is worth noting how the number of transactions varies widely between industries. We had three hundred sixty-one comps in the business services analysis, ninety-three in the wholesale/distribution analysis, and only twenty-two in the manufacturing analysis. This is a reflection of the population of businesses in each sector and consequently the number of transactions in each sector. In niche markets, comparable transactions are often hard to find, and you may have to use a similar industry segment for your comps analysis.

The sold comparables report figures do not include inventory or A/R. Inventory and A/R, if purchased, are added to the value calculated from these multiples. Note that these are added to the figure and that no multiple is applied to the inventory or A/R; these are purchased dollar for dollar. In retail and distribution businesses, the inventory value can be substantial, which is one reason a lower multiple is used for these businesses.

The bottom of each sold comparables analysis shows the sold-for price as a percentage of asking price. This is what the business sold for versus what the final asking price was on BizBuySell.com. Note that I said the final asking price. The business may have had several price reductions before it sold; there is no way to tell what the initial asking price was. While this does not give you any indication of the final selling price versus the initial asking price, it does give you an idea of how far the average seller came off of his final asking price.

One question that must be dealt with is, "what if the business has no earnings, very low earnings, or is operating at a loss?" Obviously, if the earnings (DE) are zero, the business is still worth something. For that matter, if it was losing money and you multiplied the negative earnings times the comps multiple, does that mean the seller should pay you to take it? Maybe so, in some cases. As I said earlier, comps work great if the business is in the operational norms (averages) for the industry. Comps-based, and for that matter any earnings-based, valuation method does not work on businesses that are losing money or making very little money. In general, I do not recommend buying businesses that are troubled or require a turnaround. Although you will get the business for a cheap price, it may not be a bargain when you consider the risk and additional investment involved in turning it around. Businesses that are losing money or not making much money are generally categorized as distress sales, and most brokers price these businesses somewhere between the asset value and liquidation value (see above). In general, these are not good businesses for a first-time buyer, and you would be wise to avoid them.

The comps and earnings multiple method is a great tool for you as a buyer. It is easy to apply, the results are consistent if applied properly, and you can actually see data for similar sales, which is comforting and a good sanity check. While this is a great tool, it is not an absolute value and not a formal business valuation. I have seen buyers and sellers argue over fractions on the multiple. For example, if a business had $250,000 of DE, the difference between using 2.5 X DE or 2.7 X DE for the earnings multiple is the difference between a value of $625,000 or $675,000. The methods simply are not that accurate, and many factors are not taken into account. For instance, if it is a great business, well run, great staff, excellent equipment, the seller could be right, and in fact it may be worth more. Likewise, if the business has some challenges, needs some equipment repaired or replaced for example, it may be worth less. As I said, valuation is art impersonating science. When using the comps, you need to treat the earnings multiple as an average value (which it is) and adjust the earnings multiple based on how the business compares to similar businesses. If the business truly is exceptional, then it is worth a premium and will likely fetch a better-than-average price. If the business is below average, either in earnings or operational quality, then the multiple should be discounted a bit. This is where the science departs and the art takes over. How much of a premium or discount is warranted is a judgment call. In this case, it is yours to make.

It is not uncommon to find overpriced businesses. In some cases the price comes down over time as it sits on the market. Sometimes sellers sit firm on their price and it takes a few offers well below their asking price before they realize there is a pattern and message here. And some businesses sell for a premium, perhaps substantially more than what you would pay for it. The point here is that the value of the business is an opinion. You will have yours, and sellers will have theirs. If the opinions are close, you will likely have a deal. If not, everyone will move on.

In the previous chapter, we used the earnings-value spreadsheet to recast the financial statement and determine the DE for both Acme and Way High. The earnings-value spreadsheet financial summary page has a table at the bottom where you can enter your comps data to determine a value range for the business. Let's take the comparable sales data from the BizBuySell.com sold comparables reports and plug it into the earnings-value spreadsheets for Acme and Way High and see how they look.

Acme Industrial Distributors					
Business Value Ranges					
	Comp Ranges			Value Ranges based on Last Year		
	Low	Mid	High	low	mid	high
X Gross Comp	50%	55%	60%	$417,500	$459,250	$501,000
X DE Comp	2.3	2.5	2.8	$402,500	$437,500	$490,000
	% Interest	# of Yrs	Down %	Debt Srv %	Max Value with SBA Financing	
Debt Service Check	9.0%	10	20%	35%	$503,664	

Notes — enter data in yellow boxes.

1 DE used in all calculations is the Last Year DE.

2. X Gross Comp: use % of gross sales multiple from comparable sales. Use the median or average % of gross for the mid comp figure, and select a high and low % of gross sales to see a range of values.

2. X DE Multiple Comp: use X DE multiple from comparable sales. Use the median or average X DE Multiple for the mid comp figure, and select a high and low X DE Multiple to see a range of values.

4. Debt Service Check: This is not a valuation method, it is a sanity check to see if what the maximum value is with normal bank financing and normal debt service %. The Max Value shown is the maximum total purchase price, including down payment, with these financing figures. You can change the interest %, down payment %, and debt service to look at other scenarios.

Way High Manufacturing					
Business Valuation Price Ranges					
	Comp Ranges			Value Ranges based on Last Year		
	Low	Mid	High	low	mid	high
X Gross Comp	50%	55%	60%	$750,000	$825,000	$900,000
X DE Comp	2.5	2.9	3.4	$625,000	$725,000	$850,000
	% Interest	# of Yrs	Down %	Debt Srv %	Max Value with SBA Financing	
Debt Service Check	9.0%	10	25%	35%	$767,489	

Notes — enter data in yellow boxes.

1 DE used in all calculations is the Last Year DE.

2. X Gross Comp: use % of gross sales multiple from comparable sales. Use the median or average % of gross for the mid comp figure, and select a high and low % of gross sales to see a range of values.

2. X DE Multiple Comp: use X DE multiple from comparable sales. Use the median or average X DE Multiple for the mid comp figure, and select a high and low X DE Multiple to see a range of values.

4. Debt Service Check: This is not a valuation method, it is a sanity check to see if what the maximum value is with normal bank financing and normal debt service %. The Max Value shown is the maximum total purchase price, including down payment, with these financing figures. You can change the interest %, down payment %, and debt service to look at other scenarios.

Using the wholesale-distribution comps for Acme, I set the low DE multiple at 2.3, the mid at 2.5, and the high at 2.8. This resulted in a value range from a low of $402,500, to a high of $490,000. The debt service check put the maximum value that could be financed at $503,664. The debt service check is not actually a valuation method. It is simply a quick check to see what the maximum purchase price would be if you were using bank financing. It does not take into consideration all of the factors to qualify for a loan. It is just a test to see if the deal pencils out for possible financing and what the maximum value might be. The percentage-of–gross-sales multiple is also not a formal valuation method; again, it is merely a quick sanity check to see whether the price is in the range of norms for this industry. In this case, the range is $417,500 to $501,000, which is close to the other figures.

As you can see, there is roughly a $100,000 range for the value of this business. Whether Acme would be at the high or low end of the range really depends on the quality of the business and recent financial trends. Acme has modest growth in both earnings and sales. Assuming the business is of average quality, it would likely sell at a multiple near the median, or perhaps a bit above 2.4. If the recent trends were weak, it would be discounted. If it were growing at a faster pace, it likely would fetch a premium.

Now let's look at Way High. Using the industrial manufacturing comps figures for Way High, I plugged in DE multiples of 2.5 for the low, 2.9 for the mid, and 3.4 for the high. This resulted in a low value of $625,000, a mid of $725,000, and a high of $850,000, with the debt service check coming in at $767,489. Way High is an interesting example because it has had very high growth in both sales and earnings, which will likely result in it selling for a premium. It is also in the manufacturing sector, which translates into a premium, as manufacturing businesses generally sell for higher multiples than other businesses. While Way High may be worth a premium based on industry comps and its recent financial trends, can you afford to pay this premium? Will the deal pencil out if you do?

Comps get you a market value range and provide a sanity check to confirm the price is in the right range. From there you need to see whether the deal will work for you; that is, whether it will meet your income needs and provide a reasonable return on your investment. Even if the asking price of the business is in line with the comps and your estimated market value, the deal may not work for you. If you like the business, if it meets your income needs (after debt service), and you are comfortable with the quality of the business, then this may be the one. We haven't discussed the asking price for either of these businesses yet; we will discuss that in the next chapter, where we examine both of these deals to see whether they pencil out or not. So let's see how to determine whether these deals will work.

Chapter 12: Does This Deal Work for Me?

Now that you have a value estimate for the business or businesses you are interested in, the next question is will the deal work for you. Will the net earnings after debt service be sufficient for you? Will the earnings support the financing you intend to use? Can you afford the down payment? Even if you get a business for a bargain price, it may not be a bargain if the cash flow and earnings after debt service do not meet your needs. A business can be a great deal and still not pencil out for your particular needs or situation.

So let's take a look at some ways to determine whether the deal pencils out for you. You can use the deal check worksheet from *www.mybusinessbroker. com*, or you can work these figures out on your own. The deal check worksheet has such financial ratios as ROI, DTI, and cash-on-cash return at the bottom of the page; if you are not familiar with these terms, definitions of these terms as used in this spreadsheet are in appendix 1.

Let's continue with our two example companies, Acme Industrial Distributors and Way High Manufacturing, to learn how to use the deal check worksheet. To put this into the context of an actual decision between two businesses you are considering, let's put a scenario together. Let's say you have $100,000 available for a down payment, and you need a need a net after debt service of at least $100,000. Based on these criteria, you have found two prospective companies, Acme Industrial Distributors and Way High Manufacturing. Acme is easily within your investment range, and Way High is a stretch, but you are attracted to it because of the high earnings and growth.

Let's tackle Acme Industrial Distributors first and look at it in more detail.

Overview of Acme Industrial Distributors

> Company type: Industrial wholesale distribution company selling hardware and equipment to manufacturing and industrial companies

Asking price: $475,000; 2.71 X DE plus inventory

Inventory: $30,000 (based on seller estimate)

DE: $175,000 (based on seller's claimed earnings)

Seller note: none offered

Before we start, we need some more information, such as estimated closing costs, interest rates for the financing, and what the down payment will be. For this example, I assumed you will be getting an SBA 7a loan at 9 percent interest (typical SBA 7a interest rates are prime plus 2.5 percent to 2.75 percent; sometimes you may be able to do a bit better depending on market conditions) with a ten-year term, and that the seller would be willing to carry a five year 8 percent note for $40,000 (roughly 10 percent of the purchase price).

For the estimated closing costs in this example, I used three points for the loan fees (3 percent of the loan value), plus $8,000 to $10,000 of additional closing costs (we will talk about closing costs later in this chapter); I then rounded it off at $20,000, which is close enough for this example. When you do this on an actual business you are looking at, you will need to use your best available figures and estimates to get this figure as close as possible so you don't have any surprises at the closing table.

This is how Acme looks when analyzed with the deal check worksheet:

Let's start with an offer price 15 percent below the seller's asking price and see how it looks. That would put the offer price at $400,000 plus inventory and A/R. Let's use $425,000 for the target price, and then $450,000 for the maximum price. We plug these figures into the purchase price cells in the deal check worksheet, and then plug in the inventory and A/R. The total purchase price is calculated automatically (see below).

In our scenario, we have $100,000 for a down payment, so we will plug in 20 percent for the down payment figure. The actual dollar amount is calculated automatically.

The SBA loan amount and payments also are calculated automatically, so we just need to enter the interest rate. I used 9 percent for this example, but you can plug in the current rate, which is typically prime plus 2.5 to 2.75 points (e.g., the Wall Street Journal prime rate plus 2.5 basis points or 2.5 percent).

Although the seller did not offer a note, I plugged in a small seller note of $40,000 for the offer and target, and a smaller $20,000 note for the maximum price, all at 8 percent interest fully amortized over five years, which is typical for seller notes. Few sellers will offer a seller note from the outset; you can generally negotiate a seller note when you make a written offer, especially if it is a small one, with an SBA loan providing most of the financing.

Finally, I plugged in a replacement salary of $100,000. This figure is the salary you require and is used to calculate the debt to income (DTI) and cap rate, both of which are subtracted from the DE.

Deal Check Worksheet				
Business Name:	**Acme Industrial Distributors**			
Deal Struture	Offer Price	Target Price	Max Price	Asking Price
Purchase Price	$400,000	$425,000	$450,000	$475,000
Inventory + A/R (if purchased)	$30,000	$30,000	$30,000	$30,000
Closing & other costs	$20,000	$20,000	$20,000	$20,000
Total Purchase Price	$450,000	$475,000	$500,000	$525,000
Down Payment %	20%	20%	20%	20%
Down Payment	$90,000	$95,000	$100,000	$105,000
Loan Amount	$360,000	$380,000	$400,000	$420,000
Financing				
SBA Loan				
Loan Amount	$320,000	$340,000	$380,000	$420,000
Loan Term (Years)	10	10	10	10
Interest Rate	9.0%	9.0%	9.0%	9.0%
Monthly Payment	($4,054)	($4,307)	($4,814)	($5,320)
Annual Payment	($48,643)	($51,684)	($57,764)	($63,845)
Seller Note Terms				
Note Amount	$40,000	$40,000	$20,000	$0
Note Term (Years)	5	5	5	5
Interest rate	8.0%	8.0%	8.0%	8.0%
Monthly Payment	($811)	($811)	($406)	$0
Annual Payment	($9,733)	($9,733)	($4,866)	$0
Debt Service				
Monthly Debt Service	($4,865)	($5,118)	($5,219)	($5,320)
Annual Debt Service	($58,376)	($61,416)	($62,630)	($63,845)
Stated Annual Discretionary Earnings (DE)	$175,000	$175,000	$175,000	$175,000
Annual Net Earnings after Debt Service	*$116,624*	*$113,584*	*$112,370*	*$111,155*
Financial Ratios	Replacement Salary		$100,000	
Multiple of DE on base price	2.29	2.43	2.57	2.71
Multiple of DE on Total Purchase Price	2.57	2.71	2.86	3.00
ROI (net after debt)	26%	24%	22%	21%
Cash on Cash Return after debt service	130%	120%	112%	106%
Capitalization Rate	17%	16%	15%	14%
Debt To Income Ratio - DTI	1.28	1.22	1.20	1.17

In this example you could offer, say, $400,000 plus inventory, roughly 15 percent below the seller's asking price, and the deal would pencil out very well for you. You could settle in negotiations anywhere between $425,000 plus inventory, to $450,000 plus inventory, and the deal still works. Note that your net after debt service only varies from $116,624 at the offer price, to $110,543 at the maximum price. This is roughly a $6,000 per year swing. The down payment at the offer price is $90,000, and is $100,000 at the maximum price (your maximum down payment amount for this example). So, a $50,000 increase in the purchase price only affects your bottom line by $6,000, and your down payment by $10,000.

Most banks want a minimum DTI ratio of 1.2, and some like to see a DTI of 1.25. DTI is a ratio of your debt service to your net income after your salary requirements (see appendix 1). In other words, it is a measure of the ability of the business to service the debt. The DTI ratio at the offer price is 1.28, which is well within the requirements for most banks. At the max price it is 1.20 the minimum DTI for most banks, and at the asking price the DTI is 1.17, which is just below the minimum DTI. So from a financing standpoint, this deal works anywhere between the offer price of $400,000 plus inventory and A/R for a total purchase price of $450,000, and a maximum price of $450,000 plus inventory and A/R, for a maximum total purchase price of $500,000.

What is also interesting is that while the asking price is a bit high and you would be paying a premium for the business, it actually pencils out from a net earnings standpoint. You may notice that the after debt service earnings at the asking price are roughly the same as they are for the maximum price. The reason for this is that the asking price column has zero seller financing, and all of the other columns have a five-year seller note. While the seller note is at 8 percent, which is one point lower than the bank, the term is only five years (typical for seller notes), and the payments are proportionally higher because of the shorter term. You can increase your net by using more bank financing and less seller financing, but most people like the comfort of at least a 10 percent seller note behind the deal.

Acme is an example of a business that is priced correctly, at or near market value, with numbers that pencil out well. A business like this one will sell quickly since it is priced right, has great financing available, and thus only requires a 20 percent down payment.

Now, let's take a look at a business that is overpriced and see how the numbers look when we analyze it. Way High Manufacturing is priced way high, just like its name.

Overview of Way High Manufacturing

Company type: Manufacturing company selling parts and assemblies to original equipment manufacturing (OEM) companies

Asking price: $1,000,000; 4.0 X DE plus inventory

Inventory: $100,000 (based on seller estimate)

DE: $250,000 (based on seller's claimed earnings)

Seller note: none offered

Again, we need some more information, such as estimated closing costs, interest rates for the financing, and what the down payment will be. I assumed you would be getting an SBA 7a loan at 9 percent interest with a ten-year term, and that the seller would be willing to carry a five-year 8 percent note for $50,000. Again, no seller note was offered, so we will assume the seller will accept a small note.

For the estimated closing costs in this example, I used three points for the loan fees (3 percent of the loan value) plus additional closing costs, and rounded it off at $40,000. Again, you will need to use your own estimates when you do this on an actual business.

This is how Way High Manufacturing looks when analyzed with the deal check worksheet.

The seller is asking for $1,000,000 plus inventory, which puts your total acquisition cost at roughly $1,150,000. At the bottom of the deal check worksheet, several red flags pop up. First, the DTI ratio is 1.07, which is barely enough to cover the debt service, making this a very risky loan for the bank. This is an immediate deal killer. No bank will underwrite a loan with nearly 100 percent debt service. There is too much money going to service the debt (nearly all of the earnings after the owner's salary), and not enough left to cover unforeseen expenses or unexpected declines in sales or earnings. It is just too risky and the banks won't do it, nor should you. Next the ROI is only 10 percent, which is pretty much what you can earn in much less risky and more liquid investments. Then there is the down payment issue. At the asking price, you would have to invest $230,000 to earn $110,150 per year (including your salary from operating the business), and again the numbers just don't work. The bottom line is that from a strictly financial standpoint, you would be better off investing the $230,000 elsewhere at a higher rate of return with lower risk, and keeping your job.

99

Let's say you really like the business and want to make an offer anyway. What purchase price would work for you? This is where the deal check worksheet is really handy. You can play the "what if" game and work up several scenarios, which is just what we are going to explore with Way High. So let's see what we can do for an offer and what your maximum price would be for Way High.

Let's start with the maximum price column and find out what your walk-away price is. This is an iterative process, where you take a guess at a purchase price and just play with the numbers until it makes sense and it works for you. After a few passes, I ended up with a maximum price of $850,000 and a down payment of $198,000. I did something interesting on this maximum price offer. To get to $850,000 plus inventory (a total purchase price of $950,000), I increased the seller note to $100,000, and increased the seller note term to ten years. This helped the deal pencil out better and effectively tells the seller, fine, if you want a premium I'll pay it, but you have to finance more of it. This reduces the monthly debt service and allows you to pay more for the business as a result of the better financing. Remember, you aren't just negotiating price, you are also negotiating terms, which are sometimes more important than price. Another creative way to reduce the debt service is to use an interest-only note with a balloon payment. Few sellers like this type of note, but if your seller is fixated on the price, this is a way to pay a premium and make the numbers work. As I said, if the seller wants a premium, they will have to finance it.

If the maximum price is $850,000 plus inventory, what should we use for your offer price? As I said, this is an iterative process; you pretty much start with a guess and play with the numbers until it works for you. In this example, I came up with an offer price of $700,000, a target of $800,000, and a maximum price of $850,000 plus inventory. The possibilities are limitless, as you can play with the financing structure, down payment amount, and purchase price until you find a scenario that works.

Our scenario states we have $100,000 for a down payment. However, this is a business we really want, and we figured we could somehow scrape up the extra cash since it is such an exciting deal. We will plug in 20 percent for the down payment figure since this is the best estimate for a minimum down payment; the actual dollar amount is calculated automatically. We may be able to find a 15 percent down payment or even a 10 percent down payment loan; but these are rare, so we will use the 20 percent figure for our deal check calculations.

Again, the SBA loan amount and payments are calculated automatically. We just need to enter the interest rate. I used 9 percent (the same as with Acme). You can plug in the current rate, which is typically prime plus 2.5 to 2.75 points (e.g., the Wall Street Journal prime rate plus 2.5 basis points or 2.5 percent).

Again, the seller did not offer a note. However, I plugged in a small seller note of $50,000 for the offer and target, and a larger $100,000 note for the maximum price, all at 8 percent interest fully amortized over five years, except for the maximum price note, which is for ten years.

I used the same replacement salary of $100,000. This figure is the salary you require and is used to calculate the DTI and cap rate, both of which are subtracted from the DE.

Deal Check Worksheet				
Business Name:	**Way High Manufacturing**			
Deal Struture	Offer Price	Target Price	Max Price	Asking Price
Purchase Price	$700,000	$800,000	$850,000	$1,000,000
Inventory + A/R (if purchased)	$100,000	$100,000	$100,000	$100,000
Closing & other costs	$35,000	$35,000	$40,000	$50,000
Total Purchase Price	$835,000	$935,000	$990,000	$1,150,000
Down Payment %	20%	20%	20%	20%
Down Payment	$167,000	$187,000	$198,000	$230,000
Loan Amount	$668,000	$748,000	$792,000	$920,000
Financing				
SBA Loan				
Loan Amount	$618,000	$698,000	$692,000	$920,000
Loan Term (Years)	10	10	10	10
Interest Rate	9.0%	9.0%	9.0%	9.0%
Monthly Payment	($7,829)	($8,842)	($8,766)	($11,654)
Annual Payment	($93,943)	($106,104)	($105,192)	($139,850)
Seller Note Terms				
Note Amount	$50,000	$50,000	$100,000	$0
Note Term (Years)	5	5	10	5
Interest rate	8.0%	8.0%	8.0%	8.0%
Monthly Payment	($1,014)	($1,014)	($1,213)	$0
Annual Payment	($12,166)	($12,166)	($14,559)	$0
Debt Service				
Monthly Debt Service	($8,842)	($9,856)	($9,979)	($11,654)
Annual Debt Service	($106,109)	($118,269)	($119,751)	($139,850)
Stated Annual Discretionary Earnings (DE)	$250,000	$250,000	$250,000	$250,000
Annual Net Earnings after Debt Service	**$143,891**	**$131,731**	**$130,249**	**$110,150**
Financial Ratios	Replacement Salary		$100,000	
Multiple of DE on base price	2.80	3.20	3.40	4.00
Multiple of DE on Total Purchase Price	3.34	3.74	3.96	4.60
ROI (net after debt)	17%	14%	13%	10%
Cash on Cash Return after debt service	86%	70%	66%	48%
Capitalization Rate	18%	16%	15%	13%
Debt To Income Ratio - DTI	1.41	1.27	1.25	1.07

Way High is a very interesting example, as it shows how and why an overpriced business simply will not pencil out for a buyer. We already discussed why the deal does not pencil out at the asking price. Let's see if it works at the offer, target, and maximum price.

The DTI at the asking price was 1.07, barely enough to cover the debt service after your replacement salary. At the offer price, the DTI is a comfortable 1.41; at the target price, it is 1.27; and at the maximum price, it is 1.25. The maximum price in this example really is the maximum amount you can pay, because anything above this figure won't pencil out for bank financing.

Although the deal pencils out from a bank financing standpoint at the offer, target, and maximum prices, there are some other factors you should consider before making an offer. The financial return on this business is not very attractive because it is priced at a premium, which drives your ROI figures down. There are no set minimums for ROI, cash-on-cash return, and capitalization rate; however, a basic guideline is to compare these figures to what you would earn on a moderate-risk passive investment, and then figure in an acceptable premium for your risk. For example, if you use 10 percent for your moderate-risk passive ROI, then you may want a 25 percent to 30 percent ROI from a business. The ROI for Way High is just 17 percent at the offer price, and only 13 percent at the maximum price, which is not a very attractive figure.

Way High is an acceptable deal if you can get it for your offer or target price. It starts to lose its financial appeal above the target price, and is at a premium at the maximum price figure, which in this case is the maximum price where this deal will pencil out.

Another factor to consider is your net after debt service. At the offer price your net after debt service is $143,891; at the maximum price it is $130,249. While these are respectable earnings, the offer price requires a down payment of $167,000, and the maximum price requires a down payment of $198,000. Both of these down payments are well above the $100,000 down payment criterion. You would earn a net after debt service of $113,584 from Acme at the target price with a down payment of $95,000, while with Way High you would earn a net after debt service of $131,731 with a down payment of $187,000. Basically, you are investing double the down payment to earn an additional $20,000 per year. From an ROI and financial perspective, Acme is the better deal in that the earnings are close, and the cash invested (down payment) is half that of Way High.

The cash-on-cash return is a good measure of the return on your cash investment. This is where Way High and Acme really contrast. At the target price, Way High has a cash-on-cash return of 70 percent, which means that for every $100 invested, you earn an annual net of $70 (or in this case a down payment of $187,000, with net after debt service earnings of $131,731). Comparing this to Acme, the cash-on-cash return at the target price is 120 percent, which means that for every $100 invested, you will earn an annual net after debt service of $120. Or in this case, a down payment of $95,000 will generate a net after debt service of $113,584.

One thing to take note of on the "price" of a business is the following. From the buyer's perspective, the price is the total acquisition cost. After all, that is the total amount you are investing. From the seller's perspective, the "price" of the business is the price of just the business itself, not including inventory, A/R, or any of your closing costs. In the seller's mind, the inventory is an asset he or she can sell at a profit, or worst case, liquidate and collect on the A/R. Thus in the seller's mind, the value of his or her business is what you are paying over and above the value of these assets. So in the case of Way High, your maximum price is $990,000, including inventory and closing costs. The price the seller is looking at is the $850,000 for the business itself. In fact, if Way High were a real company for sale, it is unlikely the seller would consider an offer for $700,000, which is 30 percent below the asking price, or even $800,000, which is 20 percent below the asking price, even though at $1,000,000 the deal does not make sense or pencil out for any buyer.

As I discussed in chapter 6, "How Do I Find a Business to Buy?" during your search you will run across businesses that are overpriced. The Way High Manufacturing example was designed to show you how to analyze an overpriced business and determine an offer price and maximum price for a business like this that you are interested in. As I said at the beginning of this chapter, the asking price is a starting point. You must determine whether the deal pencils out for you, will meet your needs financially, is something you can afford, and will work for you.

Many times the limiting factors for the maximum price you can pay for a business are the down payment and the debt service. Think about it. If you had all cash, you could pay as much as you wanted to. Of course, if you paid too much, the financial ratios would not be very attractive, but you could write the check and pay what you wanted. Even if you pay cash for a business or inject a higher–than-minimum down payment, it is a good idea to use the minimum down payment and bank financing as a model to see whether the deal makes sense. If the deal does not pencil out with financing, it probably is not a very good deal. Of course, there are exceptions to this. For instance, if you are buying a distressed business (which I do not recommend) or a very small business, financing may not make sense. Even in these exceptional circumstances, using the debt service model in the deal check worksheet is still informative. By inputting the purchase cost and financing terms, you will see how the business is performing financially. And even though you may be able to afford it, it may not make financial sense. There might be a better deal to be had.

While the financial considerations above are vital in determining if a deal works for you or not, there are other things to consider. These other things are less tangible and while they cannot be put into a financial spreadsheet, they must be considered. In chapter 6 How Do I Find a Business to Buy, I discussed using a scorecard to compare your choices and to rate the businesses to narrow the field. Before you write the offer revisit some of these intangible considerations now that you know more about the business. Other things to consider when evaluating the deal: will you enjoy it, is the risk acceptable to you, is the business within your capability to run after training from the seller, what is the potential for growth (if this is important to you), and how do you feel in general about the business (e.g., are you excited about it, do you find it interesting).

In addition to your down payment, you also need to consider your working capital requirements. Working capital is simply the cash you need in the bank to keep the business running and support normal operations. For a retail business, this is much lower than a B2B business, since the customers pay for their goods when they buy and you have immediate cash flow from sales. In a B2B business, such as manufacturing, distribution, or business services, most of your customers are going to have accounts with thirty-day terms, which means when you make a sale, you will get paid in thirty to forty-five days typically, and sometimes as long as sixty days. So with a B2B business, you should figure on enough working capital for sixty days of operations or whatever the cash flow for that business requires (e.g., some businesses, such as construction, get paid much slower). You can ask the seller what his typical working capital requirements are, and then add your debt service and any other costs you will have for one estimate. You can compare this with your own estimate based on typical operating expenses for the business plus your debt service. You will have a chance to look at this in much more detail during due diligence.

If any capital equipment or other major purchases need to be made within the first year, you should add this to your working capital requirements as well. Often equipment can be leased or financed, and if you decide to take this route, it will not affect your working capital requirements other than any down payment required.

In some instances the bank may be willing to lend additional funds for working capital and the purchase of A/R. Some banks will also offer a line of credit when you are doing the loan. If this is the case, you should seriously consider this, as once the deal is closed, it will be extremely difficult to get additional financing. The rule with the bank is to go the well once and draw as much as you need, and even a bit extra. Do not plan on another trip for awhile. You want to be careful with your working capital estimate, because it is easy to overestimate and equally easy to underestimate. If you overestimate your working capital requirements, it will make the deal look very expensive, and it may look like you do not have enough cash to do it. If you underestimate it, you could run out of cash and get in a jam. You can discuss the typical working capital required for the business with the seller, your CPA, and the bank to get additional input.

Below is an example of an estimate of the total cash required for a transaction, in this case Acme Industrial. The TCRE, or Total Cash Required Estimate, spreadsheet is available at *www.mybusinessbroker.com*, or you can follow this format and work up your own estimate.

Total Cash Required Estimate - TCRE			
	$ amount	%	Comments
Purchase Price (base)	$450,000		enter purchae price for business alone
Inventory	$30,000		enter inventory value/amount to be purchased in addition
A/R	$20,000		enter A/R amount to be purchased in addition if any
Total Purchase Price	$500,000		Total amount is calculated automatically, sum of above
Down Payment	$100,000	20%	enter % down payment or dollar amount
SBA Loan (if any)	$350,000	70%	Enter SBA/Bank financing $ amount
SBA Loan Closing Costs & Fees	$11,500		estimated at 3 points + $1,000, change if nescessary
Total SBA Financing	$361,500	72%	calculated total from above
Seller Financing (if any)	$50,000	10%	Enter Seller Financing $ amount
Liabilities to be assumed (if any)			Note: in most transactions the seller pays off all liabilities
Seller debt to be assumed			
Equipment Loan			
Accounts Payable			
other			
Total Liabilities to be assumed	$0		Total amount is calculated automatically, sum of above
Closing Costs			
Professional Expenses	$5,000		Your attorney & CPA expenses
Closing Costs - lender			any fees not included/rolled into loan
Escrow or closing attorney	$2,500		enter escrow or closing attorney expense
Lease Security Deposit	$2,500		reimbursement to seller for lease deposit
Other deposits	$1,000		
other			
other			
Total Closing Costs	$11,000		Total amount is calculated automatically, sum of above
Working Capital, Operating Expenses, & Start Up Costs			
Licenses & permits	$250		
Incorporation establishment	$1,500		
Business Insurance	$1,000		
Workman's Comp Insurance	$1,000		
Utility Deposits	$250		
Additional Lease deposit			
Estimated Working Capital	$20,000		estimated working capital required if not financed by bank
Other			
Other			
Total Working Capital & Start Up	$24,000		Total amount is calculated automatically, sum of above
Total Cash Required	$135,000		Total cash required including down payment, estimated costs, and working capital
Total Acquistion Cost	$506,500		All costs, less working capital & A/R

Using the TCRE spreadsheet, you can see that while the down payment is $100,000, the total cash required is $135,000 when closing costs and working capital are figured into the costs. This has turned into a big surprise for many unprepared buyers who underestimate their closing costs and working capital and overextend themselves.

In the example above we have $100,000 for a down payment and our estimated cash required turned out to be $135,000 including closing costs. Does this mean the deal is out of reach for us? Not necessarily. Most banks will roll the loan fees and points into the loan at closing and often you can also get additional financing for the purchase of A/R and sometimes working capital can be financed as well. It depends on the strength of the deal, your credit, and the bank you are working with.

Using the deal check worksheet and TCRE worksheet, you can easily determine whether a deal works for you and meets your financial needs, and whether you have sufficient cash to complete the transaction.

Acme is an example of a deal that works, and Way High Manufacturing is an example of a business with an asking price that simply does not pencil out. Assuming you have a deal that pencils out and works for you, and it is a business you like, the next step is to write an offer. Before we discuss writing an offer, we need to discus how you are going to buy the business. Will it be an asset purchase (asset sale) or stock purchase (stock sale). This is a very critical decision for you to make, and while the overwhelming majority of transactions are asset sales for reasons that will become very clear in the next chapter, it is important that you understand the basic differences between the two.

Chapter 13: Stock vs. Asset Sale

There are two types of business purchase transactions: an asset sale and a stock sale, and there are significant and important differences between the two. Most transactions are asset sales. While stock sales are less common, it is important to understand both. By the way, the stock versus asset sale question is a conundrum. Asset sales are advantageous to the buyer, and stock sales are advantageous to the seller; consequently, this is often a significant point of contention and negotiation between buyer and seller. So let's discuss each of these transactions types and examine the differences.

An asset sale is exactly what it says; it is the sale of the assets of the business by the corporation, entity, or person that owns the business. Essentially the transaction goes like this. The seller sells the assets of the company to the buyer in exchange for cash, and perhaps some debt (seller note), which goes to the seller (note that the seller could be a corporation). When we think of assets we typically think of such things as equipment, inventory, and computers (hard assets, things we can touch). These are all included in an asset sale, but an asset sale also includes the goodwill and intangible assets of the company, such as trade names, trade marks, customer lists, trade secrets, processes and procedures, product designs, and patents. All of these are assets, and in fact the value of these assets is often higher than the value of the tangible (hard) assets. An asset sale may include A/R, but it generally does not include any cash in the company bank account. If you purchase the cash, you are essentially paying a dollar to get a dollar, so what is the point. It is left out of the purchase price. If A/R is included, this asset may be financed, and you will collect on most A/R over the next thirty to sixty days, assuming it is all good and collectable (which you will verify during due diligence).

In most asset sales, the accounts payable (A/P) are paid off by the seller; however, you should not assume this is the case. Read your purchase agreement carefully to determine whether the A/P is paid off at closing by the seller, and make sure you confirm this has been done at closing.

A very important point about an asset sale is the following. You are buying the assets of the company; the old company remains intact and is still a legal entity. For example, let's say you bought Acme Industrial Distributors, which is owned by John and Mary Smith and held by the Smith Corporation. In this transaction, the assets of Smith Corporation, including the trade name Acme Industrial Distributors, are transferred to your new corporation, NewCorp Inc. NewCorp bought the assets of the company, but it does not inherit the liabilities of Smith Corporation, which still exists after closing. The cash from the asset sale transaction goes to Smith Corporation, and Smith Corporation is still responsible for any of its liabilities, including liabilities that may surface after the sale (this is an important point).

You may wonder if they paid off all of the outstanding debt and A/P (payables), what liabilities would there be left for Smith Corporation? There are lots of potential liabilities that could pop up after the transaction, many of which may be unknown at the time of due diligence and even at closing. For example, if a year after the transaction the IRS decides to audit Smith Corporation's tax returns from two years prior to the sale and finds that the company owes additional taxes, this liability stays with Smith Corporation and the owners, and is not your problem. Likewise, if an employee files a workman's compensation claim or unlawful termination claim from several months prior to the sale, again, it is not your problem; it stays with the previous corporation. This is a very important distinction between an asset sale and a stock sale, as we will discuss later.

While we are talking about employees, this is a good time to clarify a point about the employees of the company. In an asset sale, the employees are technically going to work for a new employer, NewCorp. This is a very important point, as you do not want to inherit any old or unknown liabilities. Make sure the seller pays the employees for any outstanding vacation time or sick time at closing, and have your new employees sign new employment documents. While the name remains the same, Acme Industrial Distributors (this is known as a DBA, or "doing business as," fictitious name or trade name), the new owner is NewCorp, and NewCorp is the new employer.

There are some instances where the buyer in an asset sale can have successor liability (inherit a liability from the seller). For example, in some states, if the seller does not pay the sales tax owed by the seller, the state could technically pursue the buyer for payment. This is rare, and in this example, escrow or the closing attorney should have obtained a tax release. But it could happen. Even in an asset sale, there is a risk, albeit a small one, of successor liability. Make sure your purchase agreement has representations and warranties, which is where the seller states that none of these problems exist, and that the seller takes responsibility for any liabilities resulting from the seller's actions prior to closing that may arise after closing. Also, make sure tax and lien releases are obtained through escrow or the closing attorney, since in some states the buyer (you) could become liable (responsible) for unpaid taxes, such as sales tax or employee taxes, and unpaid liens could result in you getting stuck with the seller's unpaid debts or not having clear title to things like equipment.

Another benefit of an asset sale, and an important one, is tax benefits from depreciation. In an asset sale, you are buying the assets of the company and bringing them into a new company. Many of the assets you purchase will have a tax write-off via depreciation. As a result, you get to establish the asset value of these assets for tax purposes and depreciate them on your tax returns. This is an important difference between a stock and asset sale. In a stock sale you are buying the stock of the company and essentially inherit the balance sheet and depreciated asset values, which means if an asset is already written off, you have no future or ongoing tax benefit from it. In an asset sale, you will establish a price allocation for tax purposes for all of the assets purchased. As a result, the assets the seller has owned for a long time and are fully depreciated on their books start fresh with a new asset value on your books. This a significant tax benefit for you, as you can write off the assets over the next few years. Price allocation is something you should have your CPA prepare for you, as different types of assets have different depreciation schedules (periods), and there are specific IRS rules for how the price allocation should be done. Your CPA may be able to save you some money in future taxes by carefully allocating the asset values in the most favorable way for tax purposes.

In a stock sale, you are purchasing the stock of the corporation, much like buying stock in a publicly traded company, except in this case you are buying all of the stock, 100 percent of the company. There many disadvantages to the buyer in a stock sale. Two are reduced tax write-offs and successor liability.

From a tax write-off standpoint, you are buying the stock of the company and basically purchasing the balance sheet as is. This means that you are buying the assets at their depreciated value, and any assets that are already written off have no tax benefit to you. Remember, in the asset sale you do a price allocation and step up the asset values to market value for tax purposes. In this case, the depreciation and write-offs continue at the same rate. Another consideration is the remaining depreciation life (how much longer the assets can be written off). Assets in a company have a specific and limited depreciation life, and when it ends, the book value of the asset is zero, and the depreciation (tax write-offs) stops. So from this standpoint a stock sale has a tax disadvantage to you, the buyer. While you have a tax disadvantage, the seller has a big incentive to do a stock sale. In a stock sale the seller will be taxed at the capital gains tax rate, whereas in an asset sale, the seller's tax rate can be double that tax rate or even higher! Obviously every seller that has a corporation wants a stock sale if they can get it.

We already discussed the tax implications and disadvantages for you, the buyer, in a stock sale. There is also the risk of successor liability. When you purchase a company through a stock sale, you are buying the corporate entity, and successor liability continues on with you as the new CEO, chairman, and owner. As you now own the corporate entity, you now also own any liabilities that may pop up in the future, including liabilities resulting from things that happened before you bought the company! This can include taxes, as we discussed earlier, litigation (lawsuits), debts, and product liability, such as warranties. Even with a very comprehensive due diligence, it is impossible to foretell the future with regard to what may happen and what the liabilities may be. In some companies, the successor liability may be zero, and nothing may happen; and in another, you could get surprised with a tax audit or law suit that no one saw coming during due diligence. A stock sale typically has representations and warranties where the sellers state to their knowledge there are no unknown or undisclosed liabilities, and if any occur as a result of their actions prior to the sale, they are responsible for them. Although this may sound good, if something big happens, it may be impossible to collect from them, and you will be stuck with the liability.

From the above, one might wonder why anybody would ever do a stock sale, and in fact, most choose to do an asset sale for these reasons. There are some very specific instances where a stock sale may be necessary, and in fact may be to the advantage of both the buyer and seller. If the company has contracts that cannot be transferred to a new entity (new company), then a stock sale may be your only choice in order to keep the agreements intact. In some instances, the seller's tax liabilities from an asset sale may be so high that the seller will only consider a stock sale. If this is the case, you can choose to do a stock sale, but you should recognize you are giving up substantial tax benefits (write-offs) and taking on a great deal of risk. Effectively, the stock sale is more costly to you as a buyer and reduces your future net income. The most common solution to this is to reduce the price, to compensate the buyer for the lost tax benefits, and in recognition of the seller's reduced tax liabilities. There is still the risk of unknown future liabilities and how to pay for these if something were to happen. This is typically handled with a seller note of sufficient value to cover this risk, and your attorney would write the note specifying that there is a right of offset (to reduce the value of the note) if a liability pops up resulting from seller's actions when the seller owned the business.

One of the incentives for a stock sale can be to preserve contracts or agreements in the company's name. You should be very careful, as many contracts state that if more than a specified percentage of the company's stock changes hands, the other party may cancel the contract; it also gives the other party the option of approving the new owner. If this is the driving force for your consideration of a stock sale, have your attorney carefully review these contracts to ensure that they will remain intact after the sale and that there is no, or only minimal, risk of losing the contract.

One final note on stock sales or stock purchases—it is absolutely vital that you use your attorney to write the purchase offer and that you review it with both your attorney and accountant. This is a complex transaction, with a number of things intertwined. For example, when you write your offer, it will be based on the value of the balance sheet and the earnings stream at the time of the offer. Typically, this includes such things as A/R, inventory, and A/P. What happens if the seller aggressively collects on his or her A/R (increasing the cash he can pull out before closing and reducing the value of the A/R you receive) and pays the A/P slowly (increasing the payables, debt you are inheriting)? Obviously an adjustment to the price needs to be made. More importantly, your offer should preclude this from happening by specifying minimum and maximum amounts for items on the balance sheet you are purchasing. There are many other things that must be considered in a stock sale, such as representations and warranties, due diligence, condition of the corporate entity itself, and unknown liabilities., which is why you need an experienced transaction attorney and CPA on your team for a stock transaction.

Summary of Stock vs. Asset Sale		
	Asset Sale	**Stock Sale**
Tax Benefits to Buyer	Increased Write offs & increased depreciation.	Lower write offs, same depreciation Seller has now.
Tax Benefits to Seller	Higher taxes, often double that of Stock Sale.	Capital gains tax rate, much lower than Asset Sale.
Successor Liability	Minimal successor liability.	Significant risk, little if any protection for Buyer.
Employees	Employees are new to your new corp or entity, minimal successor liability.	Continue with existing company, any employment liabilities stay with company.
Contracts	New contracts with new company.	May be able to preserve, but no guaranty, some contracts have clause about ownership change.
Credit with Suppliers	Establish new credit with suppliers, typically not a problem.	Generally transfers, unless a clause about ownership change
Lines of Credit, banks	Establish new lines under your new company.	Depends on the terms and the bank, no guaranty they will transfer to the buyer.

Chapter 14: Making an Offer

Most transactions are asset sales, and in this chapter we will assume that your transaction is an asset sale. We discussed the stock versus asset sale in chapter 13, If your transaction is going to be a stock sale, you will need your attorney to draft the purchase agreement. A stock sale, even for a very small business, has many moving parts and a number of things that must be dealt with in the purchase agreement. Work closely with your attorney and accountant on this, and before you decide to do a stock purchase, make sure you have obtained their advice. In general, stock purchases are not the best way for a buyer to buy a business. There are exceptions to this, but they are rare. With that said, let's move on and discuss writing an offer for an asset purchase.

You may write several offers before one is accepted, and even when an offer is accepted, the deal may fall apart for a variety of reasons. So, you likely will write several offers before you successfully close your deal and become a business owner. The offer is extremely important because while it is commonly called an "offer," which sounds harmless enough, it is a contract, it is binding, and it locks in the terms of your purchase agreement. So it is important to get it right and to ensure that it is complete. Once it is written, you are pretty much stuck with it, and you will have to negotiate with the seller to change anything.

Some brokers use a very informal one- or two-page offer. The argument is that it is simple, easy to understand, and the details can be worked out later. The problem with these short form offers is not what is in them; the problem is what is missing. Basically these agreements outline the price, seller note and terms (if any), training period, name the seller, name the buyer, name the brokers involved, name the escrow or closing attorney, and that's about it. It is true that the basic terms are spelled out, but as you will see, there is much more that needs to be specified and agreed to. Anything not in the agreement is open for negotiation, and you don't want to renegotiate with the seller every time something pops up. That can get expensive and can kill the deal.

Before we get into what should be in the offer or purchase agreement, let's talk about some choices for agreements. Many states have professional associations for brokers, and these associations usually have a standard asset purchase agreement form for the sale of businesses. If the broker is a member of a professional association, the standard forms are generally a good starting point (note that I said starting point). The forms for each state are different, so you will have to research this and see what is available and how comprehensive the forms are. Ask the broker for a copy of the purchase agreement or purchase offer forms for you and your attorney to review in advance. You can have your attorney review them to determine whether they are adequate and acceptable for you to use. If you can use the standard forms from the local professional association, it will save you the cost of your attorney writing one from scratch (essentially reinventing the wheel at your expense). Because the forms are standard forms, the professionals involved in the transaction likely will be familiar with them.

Remember, I said using a standard form is a great starting point. As good as some of these forms are, no standard form can cover everything, so you are probably going to need to add or modify things that are specific to your particular transaction. It is tempting get out the red pen and start marking up the agreement, but that is not the way things are done in real estate or business sales. If you need to add or modify items in the standard purchase agreement, you first complete the document, and then you write an amendment or addendum to the agreement, which is noted on the purchase agreement (usually by checking a box indicating an amendment is attached). If you need to add an item or paragraph, this is done on the amendment. If there is a paragraph on the standard purchase agreement that needs to be modified or deleted, again this is done on the amendment. The amendment is basically your eraser and Wite-Out for the purchase agreement, and you can use it to make the purchase agreement read exactly how you want it to read.

A very important part of your offer is the contingencies section. Make sure there are contingencies in the offer for anything that is beyond your complete control (which, by the way, can be a number of things). For instance, you should have contingencies for due diligence, the lease, financing (if you are using bank financing), and equipment inspection, at minimum. If the business you are purchasing is a franchised business, you should have a contingency for approval of your purchase by the franchisor and for the transfer of the franchise agreement. If you are purchasing a business that has special licensing requirements, such as a liquor license or contractor's license, make sure you have contingencies specifically for your successful attainment of these licenses.

The lease is often overlooked and taken for granted that it will not be an issue. Many times the lease works out fine; the terms remain the same, the landlord approves you to assume the lease, and it is not an issue. I have seen numerous deals killed by uncooperative landlords who seize the opportunity to change the lease terms or outright refuse to assign the existing lease or write a new lease. When you are writing the offer, there is no way to know how the landlord is going to behave or what the new lease terms will be, which is why the lease contingency is important to have in your offer. Thus, it is important to meet with the landlord during due diligence or as early as possible.

One last point regarding contingencies: make sure your contingencies require a written removal by you. Standard purchase offers and contracts used by brokers and trade associations often have a statement or clause stating that the buyer's contingencies shall be presumed to be removed at the close of escrow or after the contingency date has passed, unless the buyer has notified the broker to the contrary. If your offer has this in it, you could unknowingly have important contingencies automatically removed just by forgetting to inform the broker before the due date. This is called passive contingency removal. If the purchase agreement has a passive contingency clause or language in it, or if it does not specifically require contingencies to be removed in writing than you should write an amendment to specify this.

Once you have made your offer on the purchase agreement with your amendments, the seller may decide he or she wants to negotiate some things, such as price and terms. Again, it is tempting to mark up the purchase agreement and amendment, but as I mentioned earlier, that is not the way things are done. The seller will sign the purchase agreement and amendment (it is important that the seller sign both), and then check a box indicating "subject to counteroffer attached." The original purchase offer and amendment remain unchanged, and the changes are specified in the counteroffer. It is very important to understand that the seller has not accepted your offer, as a counteroffer exists, and your original offer is now void. You are not bound to the revised offer from the seller; you can accept it, reject it, or send the seller another counteroffer. Remember there is no agreement until both the buyer and seller have signed the purchase agreement, all amendments, and all counteroffers. By the way, your offer and the counteroffers will have an expiration date on them. If your offer is not accepted before the specified deadline, the offer is no longer valid. If the seller accepts your offer after the deadline, you are not obligated to accept it, so you can either accept it or reject it because the offer has expired. Later we will talk more about specifying expiration dates.

When the purchase offer, amendments, and counteroffers are signed by you and the seller, you have a contingent purchase offer. Why is it contingent? Because, as you will see below, your offer will have a number of contingencies outstanding, including and most importantly due diligence. What happens if during due diligence you find the earnings are lower than claimed, or you discover other problems? We will discuss this further in chapter 16, "Due

Diligence: Show Me the Money!" But basically you have three choices—walk away, renegotiate, or accept it as is. If you decide to revise your offer based on what you discover in due diligence, you will write a new counteroffer, and the broker will present it to the seller, at which point the seller can accept it or reject it. The main point here is that your offer is contingent on successful completion of due diligence and your satisfaction that the business is indeed what the seller claimed it to be.

Before you write your purchase offer, an important question to ask is who is buying it and who is the seller? First let's talk about who is buying it. If you already have a corporate entity established, then the corporation is the buyer, not you individually, and you will be signing on behalf of the corporate entity. This is seldom the case, however, as most buyers establish the corporate entity after an offer has been accepted. So, for now, you would sign personally, and later write an amendment changing the buyer from you personally to the corporate entity. What about the seller? If the business is owned by a corporate entity, then the seller is the corporate entity, not the individual. So before you write your offer, you need to know who or what owns the business.

What Price Should I Write the Offer For?

This is always a question that buyers wrestle with. Everyone wants the best deal, both you and the seller. Most sellers expect your offer to be a bit below what you are willing to pay for the business and a bit below what they are asking. In other words, they expect to negotiate, and most buyers do too. In fact, if the initial offer were accepted, both you and the seller would be wondering if you left money on the table. There is a delicate balance here. If your initial offer is ridiculously low, the seller will likely reject it without writing a counteroffer. Of course you want to get the best deal possible, and it is tempting to start with a very low price. The broker can give you some input on your initial offer, as he will have an idea of how much flexibility the seller has on the price and terms. The broker's primary objective is to get the deal done. Every broker is different; some may be very aggressive on pricing, while others play it safe. You will have to size up the broker you are working with to get a feeling for how aggressive or cautious the broker is. In the end, it is your decision as to what price to offer, and it is a judgment call you will have to make based on the value you have established, input from the broker, and your gut feeling for what the seller will accept. A good guideline is to make your initial offer within 10 to 15 percent of the maximum price you are willing to pay (note this is what you are willing to pay, not necessarily the asking price).

In chapter 11, we discussed how to estimate the value of the business. The value you calculated was an estimate and not a precise value, thus there is a range of values that could be considered reasonable. In chapter 12, we discussed how to calculate the maximum offer price, the maximum price you can offer where the deal will still work for you, your target price, and your offer price. Now you get to put that to use. Write your offer with the offer price you came up with on the deal check worksheet. If your offer price is reasonably close, say within 20 percent of the asking price, go ahead and write an offer. The seller can always write a counteroffer. If the value you place on the business is substantially lower than the asking price, you are likely wasting your time making an offer. Discuss this with the broker to see if it is worth presenting. The broker will likely have a good idea whether the seller will even consider it, respond with a counteroffer, or just flatly reject it. One thing to take into consideration is how the seller will react to your offer. If the offer is extremely low, the seller may be insulted by it. My experience has been that once this happens, it is nearly impossible to go back to the seller with a new or revised offer.

You might ask, what if the business is overpriced, and I am still interested in it? Essentially there are two ways a business can be overpriced. One way is that the seller can simply be asking too much based on the earnings, for example asking 3.5 X DE, when similar businesses are selling for 2.2 to 2.5 X DE. The other way a business can be overpriced is if the DE is overstated; for example, the claimed DE is say $175,000, and the actual DE appears to be $125,000. Even if the seller and broker used the correct DE multiple, this would result in the business being overpriced by well over $100,000, depending upon the multiple. In some cases, both the earnings may be overstated and the DE multiple used may be too high, which will result in a very high asking price.

If the DE appears to be correct and the business is overpriced because the DE (earnings) multiple is too high, your best strategy is to write your offer based on your comps and leave some room for negotiation. When you write the offer with the broker, make sure he understands the basis of your offer so he can explain how you arrived at the value and explain the comps. He is going to have to "sell" your offer to the seller, so it is important for him to understand it. It is important to have facts (comparable sales) to support your offer price; otherwise, it is just your opinion versus the seller's opinion of what the right multiple and price is, and the seller will obviously think his or her figure is right.

If you suspect the DE is overstated, there are two offer strategies you can employ. You can write an offer based on the value and DE you have calculated and explain to the broker the basis of your offer and the DE you have calculated. It is very important that the broker completely understand the basis of your offer, how you calculated the DE, and how you determined the value for the business. The broker will have to explain your offer to the seller and sell him or her on the basis of your offer. Your offer will certainly result in a counteroffer and a discussion of what the actual DE and value is during your negotiations. If the seller is motivated and reasonable (e.g., willing to look at the facts), this strategy is an effective one.

Another strategy is to write your offer for full price or something close to it (this may seem crazy, but follow the strategy a bit further). In this strategy, you write an offer that you are sure will be accepted. Your offer will state that it is based on the seller's stated DE. During due diligence, you will verify the actual DE. When you complete due diligence, you will write a revised offer based on the actual DE. This strategy is often used by professionals on large transactions and is very effective when the seller's earnings are overstated and the seller is stuck on the price. This strategy hinges on locking up the deal and getting the seller emotionally attached to the idea of closing. As due diligence progresses, the seller starts feeling closer and closer to getting the deal closed and moving on. It is important to keep everything positive and maintain a good relationship with the seller during due diligence. When due diligence is completed, you present your findings to the broker and inform him that you want to buy the business, but you are disappointed to find that the DE is lower than what was represented, and consequently the price will have to be adjusted to reflect the actual DE. After reviewing this with the broker, you write a revised offer and have the broker present it and explain it to the seller.

The only problem in using this strategy with a business owner is that the owner is not a transaction professional, has likely never sold a business before, and therefore is unpredictable. This is a very personal and often emotional matter for the seller, and even when presented factual proof that the claimed earnings are overstated, and as a result the asking price is too high, the seller may not be willing to budge on price. By the way, what happens if the stated DE is correct and is not overstated? If this is the case, then your offer would be valid. If the DE turns out to be what was claimed, that's fine. You are getting exactly what was claimed.

Overpriced businesses are fairly common. In some cases it may be a good business, and you may want to write an offer on it. The strategy you employ for your offer price will depend on how motivated the seller is, the personality of the seller, and, to a degree, the broker you are working with. Give this careful consideration before you write the offer. There is no universal strategy that always works.

You will likely get a counteroffer from the seller, and you should be prepared for this. When you get a counteroffer, it will likely be on price, perhaps a few terms, and will often clarify some points in the offer. Since you are going to get a counteroffer, it is a good idea to have some "concession" items in your offer. These are literally things you really don't care too much about and are willing to give up in negotiations. You need to be careful not to go crazy with this. If your offer is loaded with excessive demands or terms, it can be overwhelming, and the seller may just walk away without writing a counteroffer.

Some Examples of Concession Items

1. Seller training: Ask for longer seller training than you really expect or need, say six weeks, while you will be happy with four weeks. If you get six weeks, that's great. If not, no big deal.

2. Noncompete: Ask for five years, and perhaps you will be happy with three. By the way, many buyers get stuck on this and want a very long noncompete agreement. Think about it. If the seller is out of the business for a full three years and you have been successfully running the business for three years, how much of a threat will he be? Would another year or two make a difference anyway? In some rare cases it may, but in most small businesses, the seller should no longer be a competitive threat to you after a couple of years. It is also funny how sellers get stuck on this, even sellers that are retiring and really do not intend to go back into the business. Most just don't like to be tied down or locked into (or in this case out of) anything for that long, even if they really don't intend to go back into the business.

3. Seller note: Ask for slightly more on the note (higher value) and slightly better terms than you really expect to get (lower interest rate or longer note term). Again, don't go crazy on this, asking for ridiculous terms, as it can kill the entire deal. Just ask for a bit better than what you will settle for, and be prepared to accept it in a counteroffer.

4. Inventory value: This can be a tricky one, as this is directly related to the total purchase price, and lowering the value reduces your offer dollar for dollar, so be careful with this one. One way to do it is to say you will pay a maximum of $X for inventory, with X being the full or nearly full value specified, and then adding the following stipulation: Inventory purchased within the last X months shall be valued at

full value (the seller may be OK with this); any inventory over Y months old shall be valued at 80 percent of the original purchase cost; and inventory over Z months old shall be valued at 50 percent of the original purchase cost. You can negotiate the percentages and aging. The point here is that it is OK to pay full price for current inventory that is turning actively. You should not, however, pay full price for slow moving inventory, and you may not even want to pay for inventory that has not turned over in a year.

5. A/R: If you choose to buy the A/R, the seller will want full price for it, which is fine, assuming it is all good, collectable, and current. This one is often tough to negotiate. If you do buy the A/R, it sweetens the deal for the seller, since the seller gets the cash at closing as opposed to collecting it over the next few months. You can make an offer to purchase it at, say, 90 percent or 95 percent of its value, and then negotiate this with the seller. If you do purchase the A/R, make sure you do not take any accounts over sixty days past due or accounts with poor payment histories, as these are risky.

6. Closing time: Generally, the quicker you can close, the stronger your offer is to the seller. This is not a good negotiating item, since putting off the closing for an extended period generally sends a message to the seller that your offer is weak or risky. So offer your best closing time to get the seller's attention.

Many buyers get caught up in wanting to win, to get the business at their price and on their terms. If you lose the deal over a small amount of money, you did not win. In fact, you lost, and if it is a good business, someone else will buy it. The point here is to focus on your objective, buying a business, and not get caught up in win–lose negotiations. If you compromise in negotiations, end up paying a little bit more than "your price," and get a good business you are happy with, you won. And so did the seller for that matter.

Key Elements of Your Offer

So what should an offer have in it? As we discussed previously, there are many variations of agreements: standard agreements from trade associations, in-house forms used by your broker, or a custom agreement drafted by your attorney. Below is a list of key elements that should be in your offer, and a discussion of what you should consider and watch for in each of these. This is by no means a complete purchase agreement; this is summary of some of the more important sections that should be in your purchase agreement. Make sure you review the agreement you are going to use with your broker and your attorney if necessary. Many of the elements below are specific to an asset sale, which is by far the most common transaction.

1. Purchase price: This section of the purchase agreement is more than just the purchase price; it breaks down the down payment, deposit, bank financing (if any), seller financing (if any), and the inventory value included in the purchase price or purchased in addition to the price. Make sure this section is complete and accurately reflects your intentions. Any change after the offer is accepted will require a negotiation with the seller.

2. Assets included in the sale: The purchase agreement should specifically state what assets are included in the transaction. This section or paragraph should state that all assets used in the business are included in the purchase, including trade name, trademarks, customer lists, intellectual property, trade secrets, procedures, Web site, domain names (Web site addresses), e-mail addresses, phone numbers, fax numbers, franchise agreements, licensing agreements, contracts, and furniture, fixtures, and equipment (FFE). The FFE may be mentioned here in passing, but it should also have a separate section (see FFE below), as this is a very important part of your purchase. One area of frequent contention is records. The seller will need his old records for tax purposes, and obviously you need some of these records for reference and to operate the business. Make sure your agreement states which records you will get and that you have the right to make copies of any necessary records prior to the close of escrow.

3. Deposit: Your offer is not valid without "consideration," an earnest money deposit. When making an offer on a home, the deposits are often very small. In business transactions, deposits are much larger. Typical deposits are 5 percent to 10 percent of the purchase price. Never allow the deposit check to be held by the seller or cashed by anyone prior to the completion of due diligence. Your purchase offer should specify that the deposit will not be cashed until the completion of due diligence and your written removal of this contingency. The deposit should be held by a neutral third party. In some states escrows or title companies are used, and other states use a closing attorney. After you complete due diligence and remove this contingency, the deposit check is cashed, and the funds are deposited into a trust account where they remain until the closing. In some cases, you can structure your agreement for two deposits. The first deposit is the initial earnest money deposit for the offer and to start due diligence.

The second deposit is only used in cases where a very large down payment is involved. Most transactions have just one deposit.

4. Closing date: Your purchase offer will specify a closing date. The original closing date is frequently missed due to unforeseeable delays. Read the language for the closing date carefully, since every contract is different, and some may allow the seller to walk away from the deal if you miss the closing date. A good practice is to pick a conservative closing date, and if the transaction is delayed, write an amendment to reflect the new closing date. You may end up writing a couple of amendments for the closing date, but this way everyone has agreed to the new date, and you will not be in breach or default by missing the original date.

5. Contingencies: Your offer will have several contingencies, including due diligence, lease, financing, and licenses, if required. In specifying your contingencies, make sure that anything you need in order to close that is outside of your complete control is listed as a contingency. The purpose of contingencies is to protect you from being in default and losing your deposit in the event something beyond your control does not work out, such as if the landlord decides not to renew the lease or offer a new one, or after verbally giving you the green light the bank at the last minute decides not to do the deal, or if you find the business is not what you expected it to be during due diligence. If any of these events happen, you will not be able to close, and you want to be sure you will get your deposit back and will not be in default.

6. Due diligence: The due diligence contingency is the most important contingency. It is important to specify two time frames for due diligence. The first is the number of days the seller has after receipt of your due diligence list to provide the materials to you. The second is how long you have after receipt of the due diligence materials to complete your due diligence. It is important to give yourself sufficient time to do an adequate review; likewise, if your due diligence period is excessively long, it delays the closing time, and the seller may think you are not serious. When your time is up, you must either make a decision or ask for an extension if completion has been delayed.

7. Seller disclosure statement: Some trade organizations have seller disclosure statements, and they are referenced in the purchase agreement. If a seller disclosure statement is not available through the broker, you can add an addendum referencing one and either

have your attorney prepare one, or use the one available at www.mybusinessbroker.com. The seller disclosure statement is a checklist of general questions about the business. It does not replace due diligence; rather, it lays the groundwork for due diligence and asks the seller some basic questions about the business.

8. Inventory: If the business has inventory, your purchase agreement should specify the inventory value and also that the inventory will be marketable and sellable. Sometimes offers are written to include the inventory in the purchase price, and sometimes the inventory is purchased in addition to the purchase price; for example, $600,000 plus $80,000 of inventory. In either case, you want to specify the value of the inventory and also state that purchase price will be adjusted at the close of escrow based on the actual inventory value. Your agreement should specify a minimum inventory value, as you don't want the seller to deplete the inventory and leave you with nothing to sell and operate with; the agreement should also specify a maximum inventory value. Another good idea is to specify the condition of the inventory. Most agreements will have generic language that the inventory will be good and marketable or something like that. But what about its age? There could be some inventory in great condition, but obsolete or three years old with no demand. Business owners often hold on to old inventory because they hope they can sell it someday and just can't stand to throw it away. If there is old inventory, you should not pay full price for it, and in fact, you may not want to pay anything for it if it is too old and has no recent demand. Your offer should state that all inventory shall be under one year old (or pick your own time frame) and will be valued at purchase cost, and inventory over one year old will be purchased at the buyer's discretion. One more thing about inventory. Inventory is parts and materials that are sellable to customers or used to manufacture goods for customers. It is not ordinary supplies used in operations that are not for resale. If it is not sellable or used to manufacture parts that are sellable, it is not inventory. By the way, ordinary supplies and consumables used in day-to-day operations are included in the purchase price and are not considered inventory.

9. A/R: If the business has A/R, you may want to purchase the A/R. As we have discussed, there are advantages to purchasing the A/R as it provides immediate cash flow from the sales made by the seller prior to the closing. Many times the bank will finance your purchase of the A/R, which increases your working capital. The seller considers A/R

to be cash, so it is difficult to negotiate on the value of the A/R, with the exception of past-due accounts. If you decide to purchase the A/R, make sure you carefully review all of the accounts during due diligence and again at closing. You want to ensure that the invoices are real and valid, that the amounts are correct, and that they have not already been collected.

10. FFE: All businesses have FFE. In some, it may just be desks, office equipment, and computers; in others, like a manufacturing business, it may be very extensive. In either case, make sure your purchase agreement has an FFE list and that it is specific. You want to list all of the equipment so that during due diligence you can verify it is there, operational, and indeed owned by the business. You also will want to confirm at closing that the equipment is still there and operational. The list should be detailed and itemized. You may not have sufficient information to make this list when you are writing the offer. If this is the case, you specify that the complete FFE list will be added to the purchase agreement within X days of acceptance and is subject to your approval. Make sure the purchase agreement states that all FFE will be in proper operating condition and meets safety codes and industry standards at closing (e.g., if it is operational but unsafe, this should be remedied by the seller). The FFE paragraph should also state that you will inspect the equipment during due diligence and then again prior to closing.

11. Noncompete: Your purchase agreement should have a noncompete agreement. The noncompete agreement will state that the seller will not compete with you, will not approach your customers, employees, or suppliers, and will not open a similar or competing business for a specified time and within a specified distance. The noncompete agreement in standard purchase offers is usually very brief and generic, and is sufficient for most small transactions. If you have a special circumstance or need a very specific noncompete agreement, you may want to have your attorney draft one for your particular needs.

12. Training: Most standard agreements will have a paragraph on training that specifies the seller will provide X weeks of training at a minimum of Y hours per week, which is included in the purchase price. Training on small businesses is typically thirty days. Less than thirty days is generally not sufficient to learn the business well enough to be on your own, and with more complex businesses like manufacturing, you may need as long as ninety days. Sellers expect to train for a short

amount of time; holding their attention over a long period of time can be challenging (especially if it is included in the purchase price and they are not getting paid). If you need extended training, it is best to pay the seller a consulting fee and include this in your offer, or have a seller note that can serve as an insurance policy. If you have negotiated a longer training period, keep in mind that you may want the seller out early if he loses interest or starts to interfere with your transition.

13. Seller note: If a seller note is part of your offer, make sure it is spelled out in the purchase agreement and accurately reflects the terms you are offering. It is best to have your attorney draft the seller note to ensure that the terms are satisfactory to you. It is common for buyers to ask for the note to have an offset clause, which is basically an agreement that if there are any unforeseen problems with the assets or unexpected liabilities, the note will be reduced by this amount. One misunderstanding that often pops up later is collateral. Many times the seller note will just specify the amount, term (duration), and interest rate, and state that it is fully amortized or whatever the terms are. Then later on the seller will come back and demand to have collateral for the note (e.g., real estate or other assets). Sellers always want collateral above and beyond the business if they can get it. Their concern is that if you decide not to pay, you screw up the business, or you have some other financial crisis arise, they will not get paid. On the flip side, buyers don't want to provide additional collateral, as it will tie up their assets and limit their ability to borrow in the future. The buyer's thinking generally is that if the business is what the seller says it is, then that should be sufficient collateral. If you are getting an SBA loan, the collateral issue may be a moot point. The bank liens will be in first position for collateral, and if the seller wants to use the same assets, he would be behind the bank, which means the bank would collect first. Make sure the seller note in your purchase offer specifically states that the collateral for the note is the assets of the business. Another thing about the seller note is that it will almost certainly require you to personally guaranty the note. Many buyers get stuck on the personal guaranty. This is common language and is necessary, because an unscrupulous buyer could make the note in the name of a corporation and then not pay or bankrupt the corporation. The personal guaranty is just that. It is your promise to pay. As a business owner, you will have many other personal guarantees to make. Get used to it.

14. Business as usual: Some standard agreements have a paragraph stating that the seller will continue to operate the business in the usual manner, maintaining the business at its present standards and levels. The idea here is to ensure that the seller does not check out and let the business decline after an offer is made. It is a good idea to have this in your purchase agreement or to add it as an addendum, to make the seller aware of his obligation to maintain the business at is present levels and continue with business as usual.

15. Representations and warranties: This section is often skimmed over, but it is an important section. Basically this is the seller's statement that what he or she is telling you about the business is true and accurate. Typically the representations and warranties section will include the following: the seller is in compliance with applicable laws and regulations; the business is in compliance with all contracts and agreements and all are valid; there are no claims, investigations, or pending litigation; and all financial information provided is complete and accurately reflects the condition of the business. There should be a representation and warranty section, and it should at a minimum have language that covers these issues.

16. Price allocation: This is simply a statement that the buyer and seller will mutually agree on the price allocation. The price allocation has tax implications for both the buyer and seller, and it is important that your accountant prepare and review the price allocation. The price allocation will determine how you will depreciate the assets of the business and your future tax write-offs. The IRS requires that the buyer and seller use the same allocation and complete an IRS form 8594 with their tax returns, so it is important this is agreed to.

17. Employee vacation and sick time: If your transaction is an asset sale (as most are), the employees are technically going to work for a new company. Remember that you are buying the assets of the company, you are not buying the corporation itself (if it is a corporation), which is who the employees work for now. When you close escrow, the employees will now be working for your new corporation, which now owns the assets of the business you bought and the trade name. Employees don't typically understand this distinction As far as they are concerned, they worked for Acme before you bought it, and they still work for Acme after you bought it. It's just a new owner. If they have sick or vacation time on the books, it is important that the seller pays them for it at the close of escrow and that your purchase agreement specifies this. If you close escrow and the employees are

owed sick time or vacation time, you will likely be stuck giving them the time off with pay to keep them happy, even though it is the seller's liability. Make sure you check for this during due diligence, and if there is vacation or sick time on the books, the seller pays the employees for it at closing. It is best to have the employees complete new employment forms with your new company.

Some Final Thoughts on Offers

Every deal dies three times. I heard this in a seminar one time. At first I thought, wow, that is a bit harsh. Then, after thinking about it, I realized how ironically true it often is. Even the best deals run into rough spots that need to be smoothed over and hurdles that need to be cleared. Often it is delays with bank financing, or perhaps your first choice for a lender falls through (this happens even on great deals). Sometimes the landlord or lease causes a delay or even can kill the deal, or maybe you and the seller have a disagreement over something. There is a long list of things that can come up. The point is that undoubtedly things will happen along the way to closing. At the time, it will seem like the deal is dead or in serious jeopardy, but somehow these things get worked out. This is where your broker comes in; an experienced broker has probably been through something very similar before and will know how to handle it. If you approach these challenges professionally and work toward solutions rather than confrontation, you will be successful. Some deals do die, and if you have one that does, you just need to jump back in the game again.

Being first is not always best. There is an interesting dilemma with regard to first offers. Depending on the mind-set of the seller, some first offers are doomed no matter how good they are. Some sellers need to be what I call "seasoned" and see a few offers before they know what a good offer is, even if they end up turning down some good offers. This seems crazy, but it does happen. Does this mean you should not submit an offer if yours is going to be first? It depends. If the business is overpriced, and the seller seems locked in on that price, you may want to take the chance and wait for someone else to present the first offer or offers so the seller will realize that yes, it really is overpriced. You can also go ahead and submit an offer and play counteroffer volleyball, or you can submit an offer and if it is rejected come back and make another later, to a perhaps more humble seller. If the business is a really good one, then by all means jump on the opportunity and make the first offer. On really good businesses, you may not get a chance if you wait.

You will certainly have a counteroffer to your purchase offer, which means a negotiation. Every seller is different as far as how they negotiate. For that matter, so is every broker and buyer. When negotiations start, make sure you use the broker as your intermediary (remember he wants the deal to close too), and let him shuttle back and forth with the counteroffers. Make sure you maintain a professional relationship with both the broker and seller, and always focus on your objective. Sometimes negotiations can get emotional for the seller and even personal. If this happens, use the broker as your intermediary. It is the broker's job to resolve these differences and facilitate the negotiation. If you included some concession items in your offer, you can offer them up to the seller in negotiations to let him have a win; of course, this would be in exchange for something you get in the negotiation.

If it isn't in writing it was never agreed to. Make sure everything is in writing, no matter how small. Verbal agreements lead to problems later, as everyone will have a different recollection of what was agreed to. As things come up and are changed, or as new things are agreed to, make sure you write it down and that both you and the seller sign it. It is best to have the broker write an amendment or counteroffer and have both you and the seller sign it. If that is not possible, even a simple note outlining what you just agreed to signed by both you and the seller will work and may avoid a heated argument later.

You may find in due diligence that the DE is not what it was reported to be, or perhaps there is equipment that needs to be replaced and this expense was not figured into your offer, or there is something else affecting the overall value of the business. That is the point of due diligence, to determine whether the business is what it was claimed to be and what you expected it to be. If it is not, you can either walk away from the deal, or revise your offer based on what you now know. It may still be a good deal if the price or terms are revised to reflect the actual DE or circumstances. We will talk about due diligence in chapter 16, but before we move on to that, let's discuss the form of ownership for your business, corporations versus sole proprietorship.

Chapter 15: Corporations, LLCs, and Sole Proprietorship: Which One Is Right for Me?

Do you need to incorporate or establish a business entity right away? Not necessarily. Many small businesses operate as sole proprietors initially, and some remain sole proprietors throughout the life of the business. The primary reason to incorporate or establish an LLC (limited liability company) is to reduce personal liability; however, there are also tax advantages to incorporating. There is no single right answer; the right decision for you depends on your individual circumstances and the business you are buying. It is often simpler to form your corporation prior to the closing of the transaction and purchase the business through your newly formed corporate entity.

By the way, just what is an entity anyway? A business entity is a corporation, LLC, partnership, limited partnership, or whatever form the company is structured as. They are referred to as entities because they are a legal entity unto themselves, separate from you and the stockholders.

You will hear from some that LLCs are the best; others will say that "C" corporations are the best; and still others will say that "S" corporations are the only way to go. Each of these has its advantages and work well in specific circumstances. The answer is that the entity best suited for you depends on your specific circumstance and business. Talk to your CPA and attorney about your options and follow their advice. This is an area where you should not do it yourself or follow your friend's advice. It is important to get professional advice on this matter. The way you set up your business entity will have tax ramifications that could be tax benefits, or done incorrectly, tax disadvantages and costly. Whichever structure you choose, you may be stuck with it.

When discussing this with your CPA, ask which structure is best for taxes and liability protection, and ask about tax consequences when you sell the business in the future. Beware that a C Corporation will have double taxation (taxes paid by the C Corporation and then taxes paid by the stockholders on the proceeds) when you sell the business, while an LLC or S Corporation avoids this issue as they are a pass-through entity. If your CPA or attorney recommends a C Corporation, be sure you specifically discuss your tax strategy and tax implications when you sell the business. There are advantages with C Corporations, and some CPAs prefer them over S Corporations or LLCs. If you select a C Corporation, make sure you have an exit strategy to deal with the taxes when you sell the business.

Don't run off tomorrow and form your corporation. There is plenty of time for this after you have found a business. Besides, you may want to pick the name of the corporation to match the name of your business, and the type of business you buy may affect the type of corporation you establish. So this is a decision to make and an action to take after you have found a prospective business to buy. I do recommend having a general discussion about corporate entities with your CPA and attorney at this point so you can get an idea of what the expense will be to establish it and what their recommendations are. It is a good idea to shop around, as the cost to set up a corporation varies widely, and if your needs are basic, you may be able to save some money.

Let's take a look at the various choices for business structure and entities.

Business Structure Advantages and Disadvantage Summary

Sole Proprietorship	
Advantages	**Disadvantages**
+ Easy to set up, minimal cost	− Personal liability
+ Simple tax returns, schedule C	− Cannot establish corporate credit
+ Minimal paperwork & filings	− Self employment tax, limited deductions
+ Profits go directly to owner	− Tax audits more likely

Comparing Corporate Entity Types			
	C Corp	**S Corp**	**LLC**
Personal Liability	Limited	Limited	Limited
Number of owners	Unlimited	75 max	Unlimited
Taxes on profits	Corp pays taxes, up to $50,000 taxable at 15% if left in the corp, dividends paid to owners. Owners can draw a salary.	Pass thru entity, corp pays no taxes, profits/losses are passed thru to owners.	Pass thru entity, corp pays no taxes, profits/losses are passed thru to owners.
Other taxes	100% deductible health insurance,	No Social Security or Medicare taxes, may limit self employment taxes	May have self employment taxes
Deduct losses on personal taxes	No, carried forward in the corp	Yes	Yes
Taxes on sale of business	Corp and owners pay taxes on sale, can result in double taxes on sale.	Pass through; taxes on sale are paid by owners.	Pass through; taxes on sale are paid by owners.
Meetings	Board of Director meetings required, minutes, BOD votes for major decisions/actions.	Board of Director meetings required, minutes, BOD votes for major decisions/actions.	Less formal requirements for management.

As you can see, each form of corporate structure and entity has its unique advantages and disadvantages. Discuss your choice of business entity with your accountant and attorney to ensure that you pick the one that will offer you the best liability protection as well as optimum tax advantages.

Chapter 16: Due Diligence: Show Me the Money!

Due diligence is a critical step in the process of buying a business. This is where you inspect the business to see whether it is what the owner claims it to be. It is much more than just reviewing the financial statements, although this is very important. It also involves looking at the business operations, inventory, equipment, employees, customers, suppliers, competitors, and more. In a sense, it is like a well-done home inspection. You can't inspect a home by just walking through and looking at the interior and taking a quick walk around the yard. To do it right, you need to look at the heater and air conditioning unit, water heater, foundation, roof, plumbing fixtures, irrigation, attic, electrical components, and the list goes on. A good home inspection has a lot of detail to it. Ditto for due diligence. You need to really crawl around and look at the details. In this chapter, I will give you an overview of due diligence and outline the key points. Depending on the size and complexity of your transaction, and your financial knowledge, you may be capable of doing your own due diligence, or you may want your CPA to assist you with it and review the financial information. Likewise, you may want to have your attorney assist you with specific due diligence items, such as contracts and leases that will be transferred and are an important part of the business.

As you can see, due diligence is a major undertaking for both you and the seller. Both of you will invest a number of hours in this task, which is why due diligence is done after an offer has been made and accepted. This is drastically different from the corporate M&A world of large transactions, where due diligence is done before a purchase offer is presented. These transactions are so multifaceted it is impossible to construct an offer before due diligence has been done; there are just too many moving parts in these complex transactions. The buyer does not have enough information to even name a price until due diligence has been done. Consequently, on these very large and intricate transactions, a letter of intent (LOI) is prepared by the corporate attorney, and due diligence begins only after the LOI is accepted. Luckily, small and medium-size businesses are much less complex, and as discussed earlier, you can skip the LOI, write an offer with contingencies based on the information provided by the seller, and verify it during due diligence. Now is that time.

Due diligence is a crucial step, as once you complete it and remove this contingency, you are stating you have had the opportunity to inspect and review the business and are completely satisfied with it. Once you have signed off on this contingency removal, there is no going back. You can't say oops, I changed my mind; this is final, and it is a major step. Naturally, if there is fraud involved or misrepresentation, that is a different matter, and you would have to contact your attorney regarding how to proceed if you became aware of this after due diligence was completed. Of course, the whole point of due diligence is to ferret out anything that looks suspicious, and confirm it one way or the other before you move forward.

Due diligence on a very small business may be fairly simple, and it might be possible to complete it in a matter of days. On larger businesses, it may take a few weeks. How long due diligence takes is determined by how much detail you choose to look at, how quickly the seller has the complete information available, and how quickly you can review it. When you start due diligence, you must be prepared to work on this full-time. If you are still working at a corporate job, you better plan to take some time off, because due diligence cannot be done in a few hours one evening or on a Saturday afternoon.

The goal of due diligence is firstly to confirm the earnings claimed by the seller, secondly to discover whether there are any operational problems with the business, and finally to determine the overall quality of the business. With that said, recognize that every business has problems, and things that could be done better. During due diligence, you will find these problems. As I discussed in chapter 4, "Is There a Perfect Business," there are no perfect businesses. The question during due diligence is: are any of these things a deal breaker, so severe or so large that they would cause you to walk away from the deal? Finding a problem, even a disparity in the earnings, does not mean you have to walk away from the deal. If you find some issues during due diligence, you can walk away, or if you still want the business, you can renegotiate the price or terms of the agreement based on what you found.

For example, let's say you made an offer on Acme Industrial Distributors based on the seller's claimed DE of $175,000 per year. During due diligence, you found that there was an error in the add-backs or expenses and that the actual DE is $150,000. Everything else you found during your review and inspection was fine, but the earnings are $25,000 less than what your offer was based on and what you expected. In this instance, you could inform the broker and seller of your findings and let them know that you are still interested in the business, but that the price must be adjusted to reflect the actual DE. You are in an excellent position, as you can walk away from the deal if the seller doesn't adjust the price, or you can accept any reasonable adjustment offered. Some sellers won't budge, even when presented with facts showing the earnings were overstated and the business was consequently overvalued. If this is the case, you have the choice of accepting it as is, or walking away from the deal and moving on. If something like this does happen, have the broker tell the seller about your findings and discuss the issues with the seller. This will preserve your relationship with the seller, and it is easier for the broker to handle issues like this as they are a third party. This is the broker's job, to resolve things like this that come up along the way.

Due diligence is much like putting a puzzle together. You are going to be working with bits and pieces of information about the business in order to put together a picture of the overall company. You need to connect all of these pieces of information together in order to see how the company looks. If something doesn't make sense, you need to ask the seller or the seller's CPA to explain it to you. You then need to make sure the explanation makes sense, and verify it to be correct. If you aren't comfortable reviewing financial statements you may want to have your CPA help you with this. I strongly recommend buying a book on how to read and understand a financial statement.[7, 8] Even if you rely completely on your CPA for the financial review of due diligence, you need to have a basic understanding of financial statements in order to understand what your CPA is talking about. You will also need a basic understanding of financial statements to successfully run your business. You don't need to run out and buy a book on accounting, as you do not need to know how to do the accounting. You just need to know how to read and understand the financial statements your CPA or bookkeeper will be producing.

Some small businesses, such as retail, where there are a great deal of cash transactions involved, may have poor books and records. In these instances, you may have to resort to observation, which is where you literally observe the business operations over a period of time in order to estimate the daily or weekly gross sales. Observation is a very common due diligence practice with small retail businesses and even some larger ones, such as car washes. It would be nice to be able to just sit down and look at a stack of financial reports that are neatly compiled; unfortunately, with very small businesses, this information often simply does not exist. As these are very small businesses, the amount of detail necessary to confirm the earnings and health of the company is not as high since they are very small operations and are generally more straightforward.

What if the seller will not provide the information I ask for? Firstly, is the information available, and does it even exist? Many times buyers submit an exhaustive list of due diligence information they downloaded from a Web site without realizing many of these lists are intended for large M&A transactions. If the information is not available or does not exist, you need to either ask for different data or approach the problem differently (e.g., observation, or a different analysis approach). If the information does exist and the seller is refusing to provide it, this is a very different matter. First, approach the broker and let him know you cannot proceed with due diligence since the seller is not providing you with the information you requested. It is the broker's job to get this resolved. If the seller steadfastly refuses to provide you with the information you need, it is time to walk away from the transaction. If you cannot completely and thoroughly vet the financials and inspect the business, it is too risky to proceed. Due diligence truly is the time to "show me the money" and prove the financial and operational wherewithal of the business.

One thing you can do without the seller's involvement is to check for liens and judgments against the business and the seller personally. You can also independently check for complaints with the relevant local government agencies, such as police, fire, health, and code enforcement, to see whether there have been any complaints filed. A Google search on the business and the seller personally is always worth doing as well.

"Show me the money." Reviewing P&Ls, tax returns, and bank statements is a key part of due diligence. When reviewing the bank statements, you want to make sure they track the P&Ls and that the money is there. This can be a bit tricky, as the deposits won't exactly match the P&Ls due to timing and other factors. Regardless, you need to look at the bank statements and see where the money is going. Don't be shy about asking for this, since this is part of providing proof. In checking the bank statements, you can also verify the payments made from the business for expenses to see if they track with the P&L and stated expenses. Again, this won't match exactly, but it should track. In some cases, owners run personal expenses through the business checking account that do not show up on the P&L. This makes your job a bit tougher, as you have to verify all of this.

The first step in due diligence is to verify the DE, because if this does not pencil out to what is claimed, there may be no point in going into more detail. In verifying the DE, you will be starting with the P&L and tax returns, and then working backwards to verify the revenue, expenses, and most importantly, the add-backs. As we discussed in chapter 10, add-backs are a gray area where there is the most opportunity to embellish the figures, and ironically it is also often one of the most difficult to verify. You want to ensure that every add-back is directly tied to an expense category on the P&L and tax return and was actually expensed through the business. There should be a check, invoice, or credit card statement, for example, that can be directly tied to the company's financial statement. If the expense cannot be shown or found on the company financial statements, then it was never run through the business and is not a legitimate add-back. Any add-back expenses that cannot be verified should be removed from the DE calculation, which will reduce the DE and the value.

Sellers often get creative is with add-backs that are not appropriate. Below is a list of common things to look for in add-backs.

Things to Look for in Add-Backs

1. Owner's salary: This is the figure shown on the tax return and P&L. Any other figure is not correct and could be either a dividend or draw, which are not valid add-backs since these are not expensed on the P&L and tax return. Dividends and draws are taken from owner's equity on the balance sheet (much like a bank withdrawal) and are not earnings.

2. Wife, family, or partner's salary: These can be valid add-backs, but you must determine whether they are active in the business and work in the business. For instance, if a family member is paid a salary and does not work in the business and has no responsibilities in the business, this salary is a valid add-back. If a family member or partner is working in the business, then their salary is added back and replaced with a market value salary to replace them. For example, if a partner has a salary of $75,000 per year and could be replaced by an office manager earning $35,000 per year to assist you as the owner, the net add-back is $40,000 (the partner's $75,000 minus the $35,000 replacement salary, or $40,000). Salary for one full-time owner is added back. Additional owner salaries are added back, and then a market rate replacement salary is subtracted from the DE.

3. Rent: If the owner owns the building, or if the rent is not at market value, the rent should be adjusted to market rate, either up or down to reflect what the actual rent today should be.

4. Add-backs that cannot be tied to the P&L and tax return: If the add-back expense cannot be tied to the tax return and P&L, then it cannot be added back because it was never shown as an expense to begin with. Add-backs that cannot be tied to the tax return or P&L artificially inflate DE. This is an area that requires careful scrutiny on your part. Every add-back must be verified as first being a legitimate add-back (e.g., owner's benefit or nonoperational expense), and second that it was actually expensed through the business.

5. Unreported cash: We discussed this in chapter 10. If the seller cannot prove this, you should not consider it part of the income. If the seller can prove it to your satisfaction, then it is your call as to how to treat it. Many small businesses have unreported cash, and this often becomes a sticking point between the buyer and seller. If the business is a retail business, you can ask for a copy of the sales tax returns (if your state has a sales tax) to confirm the gross sales. Some businesses pay sales tax quarterly, others yearly, and a few may pay monthly. If the business is a franchise, you can also ask for a copy of the monthly operations reports filed with the franchisor. You can also conduct observation where you observe the business operations for a period of time and then calculate the daily or weekly sales.

Key Parts of Due Diligence

1. A/R and A/P: You will also want to review invoices, A/R and A/P in detail to ensure that all accounts are in order and legitimate. It is important to know the A/R are all current and are for valid invoices. It is also important to verify that the A/R shown has not already been collected on. Further, if you are purchasing the A/R, you will want to review the invoices and A/R reports again at closing to ensure that the figures are still correct and that the outstanding receivables have not already been collected. You should verify that the A/P are being paid on time and that all accounts with suppliers are in good standing, as this can affect your ability to obtain credit with the supplier when you take over.

2. Inventory purchases: Reviewing the purchases of the business is also a key element of due diligence. For one thing, this will allow you to confirm the inventory value. It will also allow you to analyze the cost of goods sold (COGS) and gross margin of the business. If the inventory value is inflated, you may end up overpaying for it. If the COGS is understated, it will cause the gross margin (gross profit) to be overstated, which will artificially inflate the bottom line earnings, resulting in the business being overvalued. Obviously this is an area you want to pay close attention to.

3. Balance sheet: Reviewing the balance sheet is equally important. This will give you some insight into the company's assets, liabilities, debt, and equity. Balance sheets can be complicated, and there is often more to the story than just the figures on the balance sheet itself. For example, to fully understand the value of the assets (e.g.,

equipment), you will need to know when they were purchased, for how much, and how the depreciation is being calculated. Remember that the asset value on the balance sheet is just an accounting figure for tax purposes; it has no relationship to the actual market value of the equipment. In fact, if some of the equipment has been owned for a long time, the value on the balance sheet could be zero, as it is completely written off for tax purposes. If you see net operating losses (NOLs), also known as carry-forward losses, on the tax returns, or negative retained earnings on the balance sheet, this may be a red flag, and you will need to dig deeper on this. Both of these point to previous losses. In the case of NOLs, the losses are being carried forward for tax purposes, and in the case of negative retained earnings, the company has not yet generated enough earnings to offset the previous losses. You should also look for bank loans and personal loans to the business from the owner or others, which can indicate the company has cash flow problems. Likewise, if there are loans to the seller, this may indicate the owner is pulling money out of the company in the form of loans. This is not necessarily a problem or red flag; it is just important to understand why it was done, whether it has impacted earnings, and what the true cash flow is for the business. If you don't understand the information on the balance sheet, have your CPA review this with you.

4. Contracts, leases, and other agreements need to be reviewed as part of your due diligence. You will want to make sure any necessary agreements are transferred to you as part of the transaction. Likewise, you want to ensure that you do not inherit any unknown liabilities should you assume any contracts or leases (e.g., lease payoff fees, transfer fees, and termination fees). You do not necessarily have to assume any liabilities, depending upon how your offer is written. The seller may be responsible to transfer these agreements to you free and clear. This is something you need to consider in preparing your offer. You will also want to review the corporate documents, although in most small businesses these are not very enlightening, as few owners put much time or detail into these. Regardless, you should review them.

5. Customer list: Verifying the status of the business' customer list is a tough one. The seller is not going to want you to contact his or her customers, as this would blow the confidentiality of the sale and could hurt the business if the sale did not go through. Yet, you need to have some idea of what the relationship is with the customers,

what the recent level of activity has been, and what the trends are. The best way to do this is to first assure the seller you will do this with absolute confidentiality; put this in writing if you need to. Then work out a way to contact the customers that will not alert them that you are a prospective buyer or that something odd is going on with one of their suppliers. One way to do this is by contacting a few key customers and posing as a new prospective customer, telling them you were given their name as a reference. This allows you to openly ask questions about the business without causing alarm. Another way is to tell the customers the company has hired you to conduct a blind customer satisfaction survey. Whatever the method, you need the seller's cooperation and permission to do this (remember the confidentiality agreement you signed), and it is important to understand the seller's concerns.

6. Lease: At this point it is too early to start negotiating a lease; however, you need to review the lease as part of your due diligence to make sure there are no surprises coming from the landlord. Your purchase agreement should have a separate lease contingency that will cover you in case you cannot reach an agreement with the landlord or the landlord does not approve you. Your objective here is to review the lease and understand the terms. If you can talk to the landlord, now is a great time to do it. Some sellers don't want you to talk to the landlord until after due diligence is complete, and there is no set rule for this. If you can discuss the lease with the landlord and get a feel for what the lease terms will be, you will have a head start and know what to expect. If you can't, you still have the lease contingency to protect you if things don't work out on the lease later.

7. Owner's role: It is vitally important for you to completely understand what the seller's role in the business is and how you will fill that role. Much of this should have been discussed in your meetings with the seller before you made an offer. Now is the time to get into more detail about what the seller's actual roles and responsibilities are.

As you can see, due diligence really is a puzzle with a lot of different pieces to be connected to get the complete picture. If you are comfortable with your ability to dig through the financial records and make sense of it all, you may be able to do it yourself. If it is a larger business with a lot of detail, you would be wise to use your CPA to review the financial portion of your due diligence. Thus far, I have outlined some of the key points of due diligence. Due diligence is a complex topic, and it is impossible to completely cover it in one chapter in this book. If your transaction is a relatively simple one, you may be able to do most, if not all, of the due diligence yourself.

If you decide to use your CPA, you can save some money by collecting and preparing (e.g., organizing) the information yourself. This will save your CPA time and save you money, as the CPA will be able to get through it more efficiently. It also keeps you involved the process. Even if you have your CPA crunch the numbers, this is not a task you should delegate completely; you need to stay involved in this from front to back. The broker is not directly involved in your due diligence. The broker will facilitate it by arranging meetings and coordinating with you and the seller; however, the broker will not be working directly with you on the review of the business itself as, this would be an obvious conflict of interest.

Typical due diligence lists do not contain a risk assessment, and while this is not part of confirming the seller's claims, this is a good time to do one. As you are grinding through the information about the company, you can to put together a basic SWOT (strengths, weaknesses, opportunities, and threats) analysis. The SWOT analysis will give you a good overview of the company's strengths, weaknesses, opportunities, and threats, which will help you during your due diligence review and will prove valuable when you own the business and start to prepare a business plan or exit strategy.

SWOT Analysis	
Strengths	Weaknesses
What are the strengths? products, employees, location, the owner, internal systems, procedures, etc.	What are the weaknesses? products, employees, the owner, internal systems, procedures, etc.
Opportunities	Threats
What are the opportunities for growth, improvement of profit or cash flow, new products, new customers, etc.	What are the threats from competitors, technology, the economy, is there a single large customer, is there a single supplier, etc.

The level of due diligence detail is up to you. The point of due diligence is to prove the earnings and the veracity of the seller's claims, as well as confirm the operational condition of the company to your satisfaction. At some point you will arrive at a point of diminishing returns, where continuing to dig and dig will shed little new light on your review. If you are pretty well satisfied and just want to be "absolutely, positively, sure," it may be time to wrap it up. Likewise, if things aren't adding up and you just don't feel right about it, as disappointing as it may be, it is probably time to wrap it up and move on to the next prospect. It would be nice if there was some sort of litmus test that could be easily applied, but there is not. In the end, it is going to be a judgment call, and that call is yours and yours alone to make.

For a sample due diligence list, see appendix 2. You can also search on the Internet for due diligence lists and get advice from your CPA or attorney. Remember, it is pointless to submit an exhaustive list containing items that the seller obviously does not have, so you will need to tailor your list to the business you are looking at. Your due diligence list will vary depending on the size and type of business you buy. For very small businesses, it may only be a few items. For much larger businesses, it will be fairly comprehensive.

Part of your due diligence should be a seller disclosure statement. A seller disclosure is much like the disclosure form used by realtors in the sale of a home, where the seller answers a checklist of questions about the condition of the home and property. A seller disclosure statement will save you some time in your due diligence, as it requires the seller to specifically answer questions about the condition of the business in writing, and it will answer some of your basic questions. Many brokers have a seller disclosure form that they will use in the transaction; if not, you can download one at *www.mybusinessbroker. com*. A seller disclosure statement or form does not replace due diligence, and it is not your due diligence list. It is just your starting point.

Steps to a Successful Due Diligence

1. Due diligence list: Compile your due diligence list, and review it with your CPA and the broker prior to submitting it to the seller. It is important to have this list ready within a couple of days after the offer is accepted, so you should be working on this in advance.

2. Timeline: Agree on a due diligence time line for how many days after the seller receives the list the material will be delivered to you, and how many days after receipt of the material you have to complete due diligence. Your purchase agreement should state that your due diligence period starts when you receive the materials from the seller.

One thing to note is that a seller rarely gets all of the requested information to the buyer on the same day.

3. Regular updates: Keep track of your progress, and update the broker and seller regularly. If you are missing information, make sure you let them know, and as items are completed, keep them informed of this as well.

4. Work at it full-time: Due diligence is a critical step in the process, and it is important that this task has your full attention. It is also a time-consuming task requiring significant investment and commitment of your time. Even if you use your CPA to assist you, you must be fully committed and fully available to work on this.

5. Ask questions: If you run into a snag and something is not making sense, ask the seller or the seller's CPA to explain it. Make no assumptions.

6. Focus on key points: Countless small things will come up during due diligence, and it is easy to get sidetracked on these. You need to decide what is truly important and relevant to determining the financial strength and operational quality of the business, and focus on these important points.

7. Review meetings: Some items on your list may need to be handled via an interview with the seller or may require the seller to explain the information to you. Be considerate of the seller's time, since the seller still has a business to run while you are doing this. Be as efficient as possible, keeping these meetings to as few as possible, and keeping them focused, on track, and as short as possible.

8. Keep a list of what you find: As you review your due diligence items, keep a running list of what is completed, what the results were, and what actions are required if any.

9. Schedule a final review meeting: When you are finished, schedule a final review meeting with the seller, and the seller's CPA if necessary, to wrap things up. If you have decided the business does not meet your expectations and you are going to pass, there is no need for this meeting, unless you feel there may be a way to resolve your concerns.

10. Sign off or move on: When your due diligence is complete and you are completely satisfied, it is time to sign the contingency removal form and move to the next step, typically opening escrow. This is a major step, and there is no going back. Likewise, the deal does not go

forward until you sign off on due diligence. If things aren't looking good and you aren't comfortable with what you are finding, it is time to move on. If you have to move on, let the broker know you are not satisfied with the results of the due diligence and have him inform the seller. This is the broker's job and not yours. One thing to note about this is that you do not have to defend your decision to move on, and you do not have to prove the results of your review. This is your decision and your decision alone. If you need more time, you can always ask for an extension, and if the seller agrees, due diligence can be extended for a reasonable amount of time. Most sellers will agree to this if things are going well, albeit slower than expected (sometimes due to a delay in seller's materials being available). One thing to watch for is a passive contingency removal, which is a statement saying that due diligence will be presumed to be acceptable to the buyer after X days unless the buyer notifies the broker in writing to the contrary (or something like this). Passive contingency removals are fairly common in standard contracts from brokers and trade associations. If your agreement has this in it, I highly recommend you write an amendment stating that the due diligence contingency requires your written approval to be removed. If not, make sure you remember to notify the broker one way or the other on the due date, and put it in writing to be safe.

Let's take a look at a due diligence success story that could have easily turned into a deal killer.

Careful Due Diligence Saved this Buyer Money

Pete made a very reasonable offer for a small franchised restaurant that was being run by the two brothers. It was their mother's business, and she had recently died. The brothers were running the pizza restaurant while working their regular jobs until it could be sold. The brothers accepted the offer. Pete completed his due diligence and found a significant problem. Royalty payments had not been made for several months, totaling over $25,000, which caused the expenses to be understated; consequently, the DE was inflated by this amount.

Everything else was pretty much in order. Pete really liked the restaurant and wanted to conclude the deal, but with the reduction in earnings, it was now overpriced.

Pete considered his options with his broker, which were to inform the seller of the discrepancy and walk away from the deal, accept it as is, or make a revised offer based on the new information. Pete decided to make a revised offer at a substantially lower price. While this was disappointing for the brothers, the reality was that it was a fair offer and likely as good as any future offer they would get based on the reduced DE (earnings). Pete had the strategic advantage in that he could close immediately, and the brothers did not want to continue operating the business while working their other jobs. The brothers accepted the offer, and Pete bought the pizza restaurant for a great price.

Patience and Professionalism Pays in Due Diligence

Brian and his partner Allen made an offer on a security business and were ready to start due diligence. Brian had a background in the security business and new the business very well; Allen had a financial background and was going to take the lead on the financial aspect of the due diligence while Brian handled the operational part of it. They started due diligence with a fairly comprehensive list of things they wanted to review. Their list was reasonable and the seller was very well organized and well prepared, so due diligence started off well. Brian and Allen were pros and very thorough. The seller ran the business well and had very good books and records, so the process went smoothly.

Along the way there were discrepancies that surfaced. Brian and Allen took a very professional approach to each discrepancy they found. They never accused the seller of misstating the figures or inflating the earnings. With each discrepancy they found they went back to the seller through the broker and asked the seller to explain the discrepancy to them. As this was an exceptionally well run business with great books and records, nearly all of the discrepancies could be explained and the DE turned out to be what they expected. When Brian and Allen found minor discrepancies they moved on if they were not important and they focused on the key items and major areas of concern. Brian and Allen bought the business and maintained an excellent relationship with the seller through training and after training.

While the business in this example was exceptionally well run with great books and records, it is an example of how due diligence should go and how it should be done. Both the buyers and sellers were very professional and courteous to each other throughout the due diligence process. Brian and Allen were very reasonable in their expectations and applied a very pragmatic approach to their due diligence.

Now let's move on to the actual transaction process and see how a deal comes together from beginning to a successful purchase.

Chapter 17: The Transaction Process: 30 Steps to a Successful Acquisition

The typical transaction process is shown below. This process will vary slightly from state to state, as some use escrows for closing, while others use a closing attorney; but in general, the transaction will follow these steps. It will also be different if you are purchasing a FSBO business, as there will not be a broker involved. One might think this would simplify the process, as you are working directly with the seller, but actually the opposite is true, since the seller typically has no idea how to do the transaction. Consequently the process is random at best, and often fluid (constantly changing) at worst, and there is not an experienced professional involved to keep things on track. If you are purchasing a FSBO, make sure the critical steps are followed, and make sure you have consulted with your attorney to ensure that the transaction is being handled properly.

30 Steps to a Successful Acquisition

1. Preparation and commitment: It starts with your decision and personal commitment to buy a business. Buying a business is a major undertaking requiring a major commitment of your time and the dedication to stick with it, as it generally takes a while to find the right business. You will also need to have the funds ready to invest for the down payment, and the necessary working capital.

2. Search for prospective businesses; your first pass: Start your search by just surfing through such Web sites as, *www.vrbusinessbrokers. com*, *www.bizbuysell.com*, and *www.bizquest.com* just to see what is available. While you are looking at these businesses, consider the following: which ones interest you, which ones are in your price range, and which ones are the best fit for you. Take note of local brokers with the best businesses (not necessarily the most) for sale.

3. Narrow and refine your search: There are many businesses available; in fact, far too many to be able look at every one, even in a single city.

Select a few of the best prospects to focus on, print out the ad pages, and make a list.

4. Contact the broker (or owner if a FSBO): You can click on the link on the Web site to contact the broker, who will send you a confidentiality agreement. If it is a FSBO, the sellers will respond directly. With FSBOs, the process is somewhat random on the sellers' end, as most likely they are not professional intermediaries, and they probably have not done this before; so they are pretty much winging it on their end. You can also call the number on the ad and ask the broker a few questions. Remember, brokers will not get into any detail until after you have signed a confidentiality agreement, but you can ask a few basic questions to see whether you want to look at the business in more detail. From this point on, I will assume you are working with a broker. If you are working with a FSBO, you can do your best to follow these steps (see chapter 8).

5. Confidentiality agreement and buyer profile: The next step involves signing a confidentiality agreement, completing a buyer profile, and sometimes providing a personal financial statement. The broker will require these documents before sending any confidential information to you. If you have a resume and personal financial statement, this information is very helpful and may be required on high-value businesses prior to receiving any confidential information. Likewise if you intend to get an SBA loan, the bank will require a resume and personal financial statement on an SBA 413 form.

6. Business profile: The broker will send you confidential business profiles for the businesses you are interested in. The business profile has a summary of the business, financial information, and facility and lease information, among other things. On larger businesses, the profiles will be very comprehensive; on smaller ones, the profile may be simply a one-page or two-page summary.

7. Review the business profiles: Review the business profiles, and make notes of questions you have about the business. Many of your basic questions can be answered by the broker over the phone. This is not the time to dig into exhaustive detail on the financials, and it is not the time to challenge the accuracy of the information. No doubt you will have questions, and some of the information may not make sense at this point. For now, note your questions, and clear up as many as possible with the broker. If you are interested in the business, you will have the opportunity to meet the seller to learn more about the

business and get to the next level of detail. At this point, you are just narrowing your list of prospective businesses.

8. Meeting with sellers: Once you have your short list of a few businesses to look at, contact the broker to set up a meeting with the seller. This meeting gives you the opportunity to ask questions about the business directly to the seller, as well as describe your qualifications to the seller. It is important to keep the meeting with the seller focused and on track and not to waste time on obvious or redundant questions (be respectful of the seller's time; see chapter 9).

9. Evaluate your choices: After your meeting, evaluate the businesses you have looked at. Are any of these the right one? Would you be happy with one of these businesses? Do any of them meet your criteria? You can download the business evaluation scorecard at *www. mybusinessbroker.com* to help you evaluate your choices and weigh your decision. If you have found a good prospect, move on to the next step to see if the deal will work for you; if not, go back to step 2 and continue your search until you find a good one. You will likely ride this merry-go-round for awhile to find the right business. Be patient. The right business is out there for you.

10. What's it worth to me: Once you have found a business or a couple of businesses you may want to make an offer on, it is time to see whether the price makes sense and what it is worth to you. You can use the earnings-value worksheet from *www.mybusinessbroker.com* to analyze the DE for the business and plug in comps to calculate market value ranges (see chapter 11).

11. Does this deal work for me? Decision time: Before you make your final decision and write an offer, make sure the deal works for you. Crunch the numbers based on the information available (remember you will verify the numbers during due diligence), and make sure the earnings after debt service will meet your needs. Most importantly, make sure that this is the business you want and that you will be happy owning it. You can use the deal check worksheet from *www. mybusinessbroker.com* and the steps we discussed in chapter 12 to determine whether the deal makes sense for you and whether it will meet your income needs after debt service.

12. Offer to purchase: Your broker will write a purchase offer (most likely on the broker's standard forms) and help you write any addendums and the contingencies. Your offer will include an earnest money deposit check, and such contingencies as books and records proving out (due

diligence), a lease contingency, and a financing contingency. Your earnest money check is typically not deposited until due diligence is completed and escrow is opened. Make sure you carefully review the purchase offer and that it accurately reflects your intended offer. Also, make sure the essential elements we discussed in chapter 14 are in the purchase offer or addendums. Have your attorney review the agreement prior to signing it if you are unsure about any of the terms and conditions.

13. Present offer: The broker will present your offer to the seller, and will explain the terms and conditions of your offer to the seller and other decision-makers. The broker will also provide the seller with your background information, financial qualifications, and experience. Favorable background information eases the seller's concerns about your credit worthiness, your ability to successfully operate the business, and most importantly, your ability to close the deal.

14. Acceptance or counteroffer: The seller either accepts the offer as it is written or writes a counteroffer. You will likely get at least one counteroffer, typically on price and some of the terms, and clarifying some points in the offer. When you and the seller agree to all terms and conditions of the sale and sign all counteroffers and amendments, it then becomes a contingent purchase agreement.

15. Due diligence and inspection: You meet with the seller to examine the financial records and conduct other reviews that are part of the due diligence process. This is a critical step where you examine the business to ensure that it is what the seller claimed it to be and that it meets the conditions of your offer. Chapter 16 discusses due diligence in more detail, and appendix 2 has sample items typically requested during due diligence. You will need to tailor your list for the specific business you are looking at.

16. Contingency removal: You remove your contingencies as each is completed or met to your satisfaction. It is best to remove each contingency in writing. Likewise it is important to request an extension to the due diligence period, if necessary, in writing and also to notify the broker and seller in writing of any problems. If at the end of the due diligence period the business does not meet your expectations you have three choices: 1) notify the broker in writing that after your due diligence review you are not satisfied with the business and consequently do not intend to proceed with the transaction and are hereby requesting the contract be terminated

and your deposit returned, 2) notify the broker, in writing, of the issues or concerns and request a meeting to answer your questions and resolve the outstanding issues with the seller and broker (note that it is best to put these concerns and issues in writing to the broker so the seller can prepare and respond properly), 3) notify the broker, in writing, that based on your due diligence review a revised offer is necessary before you can proceed. It is important to explain what the basis of the revised offer is and what issues you found during due diligence so the broker can properly present and explain your revised offer.

17. Escrow: After you complete due diligence and remove the due diligence contingency, the broker (or the closing attorney) will open escrow (note that some states do not use escrows, I have used the term "escrow" for this stage of the closing process as it is a familiar term to most). The broker sends the purchase agreement and other documents to escrow (or the closing attorney), and escrow draws the escrow documents and deposits your earnest money deposit check in the trust account. Escrow is "open" as soon as both the buyer and seller have signed the escrow documents and returned them to escrow. It is very important to note that nothing moves forward until both the buyer and seller sign these documents. To keep the transaction moving forward in a timely manner, make sure these documents are signed promptly.

18. Buyer to-do list: Business license, business insurance, workman's comp insurance, EIN (employer identification number) or TIN (tax identification number), establishing a corporation, licensing if required, establishing a bank account, etc. During the escrow period, you will be very busy getting all of your licenses, permits, insurance, and legal documents in order. Review your list with the broker, seller, and escrow/closing attorney to make sure you have a complete list of everything you need in order to close. It is important to start work on this immediately, as some of these items can delay the close of escrow if they are not completed on time. So start early; there is much to do.

19. Bank documents: If you are getting an SBA loan, there will be information required from both you and the seller. The loan approval process does not start until *all* of the documents from both you and the seller are submitted to the underwriter for review. Closings are often delayed because the bank is not ready to fund, and the delay is almost always a result of the paperwork not being submitted to

the bank promptly; the paperwork being submitted incorrectly; or the paperwork being submitted incomplete. It is critical to get all of the documents and information to the bank immediately. This is your highest priority after your offer is accepted and due diligence is complete, as loan approval and funding generally take the longest out of all of the items required to close. Another important reason to get the loan approval process going as soon as possible is the risk that the bank may not approve the deal and if this happens you need to know early so you can find another bank. This is why bank financing is one of your contingencies, just in case this occurs. If it does, make sure you request an extension to the closing date in writing.

20. Lease assignment/new lease: The seller's landlord may require the assignment of the existing lease or a new lease. You will work with the seller and the landlord to obtain a lease or lease assignment. This is a critical step and one of your remaining contingencies. It is important to provide the landlord with a complete personal financial statement, resume, and lease application promptly. The landlord will make his or her decision on your lease approval, and even terms, based on your financial qualifications and business experience. It is important to provide the landlord with a very positive image of both your financial strength (ability to pay the rent, and credit worthiness) and your business experience (ability to successfully operate the business).

21. Lien search: Escrow officer checks for liens against the business and its assets, gets releases from secured creditors, and checks with state and federal agencies for tax clearances. You want to ensure that this is being done. Ask your escrow agent or closing attorney about this. At your request, escrow or the closing attorney will process the fictitious name or DBA filing for you.

22. Note and lease assumptions: If there are any notes or leases (e.g., equipment leases) to be assumed by you, you will work with the seller and the escrow officer to process the documents to assume these notes or have equipment leases assigned to you. Be very careful about assuming any notes or leases. Make sure you clearly understand the terms, conditions, and amounts you are assuming. It is generally easier and less risky to have the seller pay off all liabilities at the close of escrow.

23. Price allocation: If your transaction is an asset sale, and most are (see chapter 13), a price allocation is required by the IRS. The Price allocation is used for tax purposes to specify how the purchase amount

is divided between different assets, such as equipment, goodwill, and noncompete agreements. Each of these has a different depreciation schedule (write-off time), and some are more favorable than others. There are strict IRS rules associated with this, and you should have your CPA either prepare or review the price allocation to ensure that it complies with these requirements. You will need to file an IRS form 8594 with your tax return at the end of the year.

24. Inventory: You and the seller take inventory (if it applies to your business). If it is a large or complex inventory, it may be necessary to use an inventory service. Inventory should be counted as close to the closing date as possible in order to get an accurate count and value of the inventory you are purchasing. It is best to discuss how the inventory count will be handled in advance with the broker and seller, and to develop a plan as well as an agreed method for valuing the inventory. Discuss in advance how old inventory will be valued (e.g., inventory over twelve months old or inventory with no recent demand and transaction history). Sellers almost always want full value for the entire inventory, even old and obsolete inventory. Current inventory is worth full value, but you should not pay full value for inventory with no recent demand.

25. FFE inspection and final walkthrough: You should conduct a prelimary FFE inspection either during due diligence or immediately after opening escrow and notify the broker and seller of any discrepancies or equipment in need of repair. You should do a final inspection of the equipment and premises just before closing. Make sure the purchase agreement specifies this and that the seller is aware of this in advance (this is the broker's job, but it is best to make sure that the seller is expecting the inspection and that it is not a surprise).

26. Closing, COE (close of escrow): The signing of the final closing documents may be done at escrow, in person, or, in many cases, via e-mail or fax. Change of possession (COP) is typically done at the same time as COE; however, this is not always the case. In some instances, COP may take place in advance (early possession) if unforeseen things delay closing (e.g., bank funding or documents) and both parties agree to it.

27. Congratulations! You are a business owner!

28. Training: Your training with the seller commences after the close of escrow and at COP, and continues for the period specified in your purchase agreement. During this time, it is important to remember

that the seller is very proud of his or her business and the way it runs. This is not the time to implement your improvements or start changing the way the business runs, as this can damage your relationship with the seller, which you need to preserve and maintain during training. It is best to wait to make your improvements and changes until you have a complete understanding of the business and the seller is no longer involved. For now, watch and learn. Be a sponge and soak up everything you can from the seller. By maintaining a courteous and professional relationship with the seller, you will have a cooperative trainer teaching you everything he or she knows about the business. By maintaining this relationship, you will be able to call the seller after the training period is over with questions if necessary.

29. My 100-day plan: Your 100-day plan is your transition plan from the seller's ownership and leadership to yours. Chapter 19 discusses developing your 100-day plan.

30. My first-year plan and exit strategy: After successfully wrapping up your training and first one hundred days, it is time to start thinking longer term. You now know enough about the business to develop a plan for your first year, and your exit strategy. Chapters 20 and 21 discuss developing your first-year plan and your exit strategy, respectively.

Additional Thoughts About the Transaction Process

The business-search merry-go-round. You will go through steps 2 through 9 above (searching for prospective businesses) several times. There is no way to shortcut the process. In order to find the right business, you will have to look at a number of prospects. This is part of the journey to finding the right business. There will be many stops along the way. You will review lots of business profiles and meet with a number of sellers before you find the right business. For some, this process takes months, and for others, it can take a year or more. It depends upon the type of business you are looking for, how narrow or broad your search is, and how much time you dedicate to your search. The process can be fun; you will meet some interesting people, see a wide variety of businesses, and learn a lot along the way. Be patient, keep an open mind, and enjoy the journey.

Some buyers have asked, "Do I have to use an escrow or closing attorney?" because they want to save some money. It is very important to use either an escrow or closing attorney. The escrow officer or closing attorney performs a number of very important tasks, and most importantly, is the neutral third party holding and distributing the funds. As a neutral third party, the escrow or closing attorney ensures that all of the paperwork is signed and executed properly and that no money is distributed without agreement by both the buyer and seller. If the deal falls apart, your money is being held by a neutral party, not the seller or the seller's attorney. Does this mean that if you change your mind or something goes wrong the escrow or closing attorney will just send your money back? Not a chance. Both you and the seller have signed a contract. The contract will have a number of contingencies in it which you will remove step by step as the transaction progresses to your satisfaction. Once you have completed due diligence and remove this contingency, you are giving the deal a green light, stating that you are satisfied with the business. It is at this point that escrow is opened. There are still other contingencies and many things to do before the closing, and yes, if something goes wrong you can get your deposit back less the escrow fees as long as it is covered by one of the remaining contingencies. Remember, you have signed a contract, basically have promised, to close the deal as long as your contingencies are met and satisfied.

The escrow or closing attorney is a neutral third party; the attorney does not take sides and cannot favor anyone. If the deal collapses for any reason, the escrow or closing attorney needs the agreement and signatures of both the buyer and seller before any money can be distributed to either side. Your money stays in escrow. The business is still under contract and in escrow until everything is settled to the satisfaction of both buyer and seller. So if something goes wrong, everything goes on hold until both sides sort it out. This protects both you and the seller.

Opening escrow is a major step. While there are likely still contingencies remaining for the lease, financing, and possibly other things, you have signed off on the due diligence contingency, which is stating that you have inspected the business, reviewed the books and records, and are satisfied with the business itself. This is a very important step, as once you have signed off on due diligence, it is very difficult to come back and say you aren't happy with the financial condition of the business or the books and records. You have already stated in writing that you reviewed this information and were satisfied with it. The exception to this is if you later discover that the information provided was incorrect, or that information was withheld from you. In this case you should discuss the situation with the broker and your attorney.

As long as there are contingencies remaining open (e.g., lease, financing), you are not completely locked into the deal. Should the lease or financing fall through for reasons beyond your control, your deposit should be returned less any fees, such as escrow that may be due. If you change your mind after opening escrow and removing contingencies, you will likely lose your deposit and could be at risk of being in breach of the contract. Consult the broker and your attorney before opening escrow and before removing any contingencies.

As you can see, the purchase agreement increasingly binds you as the contingencies are removed. It also binds the seller and prevents the seller from changing the price and terms, or even changing his or her mind. This may seem crazy, but on occasion it does happen. If it does, the purchase agreement and escrow also binds the seller and protects you. You actually have a great deal of flexibility, as you have contingencies in the purchase agreement and the seller does not. So you have opportunities to walk away if things go wrong, and the seller has very limited ways to get out of the deal.

Chapter 18: Closing and What's Next

You made an offer, it has been accepted, you've successfully completed due diligence, all of your buyer to-do's are done, and you are just about ready to close escrow or sign the closing documents with the closing attorney. This is it—just one more step and you are a business owner! Let's go over the preclosing checklist, final things to do at closing, and discuss what happens next.

1. Business condition: Just before closing you should verify that the business is still operating the same as it was during due diligence. You'll want to verify that sales are on track, no major customers have been lost, there has been no change in supplier relationships, and there are no changes in the staff pool. Essentially, you want to ensure that there have been no adverse changes in the condition of the business.

2. A/R: If you are purchasing the A/R, it is important to verify the A/R value and condition, and confirm that the accounts have not been collected.

3. A/P: Confirm that the suppliers have been paid by checking invoices, and make sure you have new accounts established (you do not want to get stuck with the seller's bills).

4. Insurance: Make sure your business insurance (liability and other insurance) and workman's compensation insurance is ready for the close of escrow.

5. Lease: Make sure you have a signed lease or a lease assignment from the landlord.

6. Utilities: Have your utility accounts (electric, phone, etc.) ready for the closing.

7. Website and e-mail: Make sure the Web site and e-mail accounts are transferred to you.

8. Tax ID: You will need a tax ID (i.e., an EIN or a TIN) if you have established a corporation.

9. Corporate documents: If you have established a corporation or LLC, you will need your corporate documents well before the close of escrow, for the closing and for the bank if you are using bank financing (SBA).

10. Copies of records: Some sellers are reluctant to turn over all of their records, and they do need financial records for their taxes. To ensure that this does not turn into a conflict, make sure that your purchase agreement specifies you can make copies prior to the close of escrow, that the seller is aware of this in advance, and that you only ask for the records you need to run the business.

11. Lien and judgment search: Make sure the escrow or closing attorney has performed a lien search and that tax releases have been obtained from state and federal agencies. Also, check leases on equipment to ensure that they are paid off or transferred as specified in your agreement.

12. Inventory count: You reviewed the inventory during due diligence, and now it is time to do a complete and accurate count. This is important to do right before closing, as the inventory figure you and the seller agree on will be inventory value you pay for. It is important not only to count the inventory, but also to confirm the quality and aging of the inventory if you have not already done so. Make sure you and the seller have agreed on how the inventory will be valued (e.g., how will older inventory be valued).

13. FFE: You already inspected the FFE during due diligence, and now it is time to confirm that all of the FFE is in the same condition and still there.

14. Final deposit: If you have a final cash deposit due to escrow, make sure your funds are ready. Escrow will want either a cashier's check or wire transfer; otherwise closing is delayed until the check clears. Even with a cashier's check or wire transfer, you should plan on sending it to escrow the day before closing or first thing in the morning to ensure that it arrives in time for closing.

15. Bank financing: Final loan approval and funding is often the last item required for closing. Most banks will fund a loan within three days after final approval and after the loan documents have been signed. Make sure you get all of your paperwork to the bank as quickly as possible and follow up with the bank weekly to check progress and status.

16. Bank accounts: Your new bank accounts will need to be established before the close of escrow.

17. Licenses and permits: Depending upon the type of business, you may need licenses and permits to operate. Make sure you have all of the necessary licenses and permits prior to closing. It is best to check on this during due diligence to make sure you know what licenses and permits are required, what is required to obtain them, and how long it will take.

18. Training: Make sure you have discussed training with the seller and that the seller has agreed to a specific schedule.

Congratulations! You are a business owner! With the above completed, you are ready to sign the final documents, close escrow, and start training with the seller.

Chapter 19: My 100-Day Plan

Now that it is your business (congratulations again!), you get to step in and do things your way, fix all of those obvious problems you found, add those new products or services you thought of, and prepare for the business to really take off! Right? Well not just yet.

The first order of business after the closing is training. Your purchase agreement will have specified a period of weeks and hours per week for seller training. Two important things to recognize are that while you are excited about your new business, the seller is starting to check out mentally, as he or she just sold it and is eager to move on to whatever is next. Secondly, keep in mind that the seller is very proud of his or her business, and during training will likely still feel a sense of ownership and feel somewhat in charge. It is very important to maintain a professional and cordial relationship with the seller through training and beyond. You will need the seller's full cooperation during training in order to learn about the business, and you may need to call the seller later for advice or even assistance. This does not imply that you are "working for the seller"; you just need to be aware of the seller's emotional attachment and connection to the business during the transition period. It is very important to keep the seller engaged and committed during training so you can absorb as much information as possible. It is important to make sure that the seller meets his or her commitment for training, that he or she shows up every day, and that he or she works directly with you to complete the training. Although you have specified training in the purchase agreement, it is also important to remind the seller, during due diligence and when closing, how important training is to your success.

Of course, you are excited about your new business and naturally want to step in right away and do it your way and make it your business. You may have some very good ideas, yet it is best to hold off on making any changes, unless they are urgent, for the first few weeks. Some things the former owner did may seem crazy or unnecessary, but after your training period and after running the business for awhile, they may make sense. It is important to go slowly with changes until you fully understand the business and the reasons why things are done the way they are. If you bought a good business and it was making money, then it is running reasonably well. While there is always room for improvement, it is critical to develop a good understanding of the business before you start making changes.

Another reason to wait to make any changes is the employees. Employees are always very nervous when a business is sold and a new owner steps in. Rumors fly that everyone is going to lose their job, that the business is in trouble and that's why the owner sold it, or that everything is going to change now. Your employees are critical to the success of your new business, and it is important to reassure them that their jobs are secure, that they will enjoy working for you, and that the business is going to pretty much remain the same. This doesn't mean you can never make changes, but it does mean you cannot step in on day one and start a major business overhaul. When you do start to make changes, implement them slowly and with the consensus of the staff. You want them to understand where you are taking the business and why you are making the changes so you can obtain their support. A transition meeting with the previous owner, you, and the staff just before closing or immediately after closing is very important. People don't like surprises or change, and this is both. So it is important to understand the concerns of the staff and make them feel comfortable with you, the new owner, and secure in their jobs.

Suppliers are a very important part of your transition plan. During due diligence, you should have reviewed the suppliers and the supplier relationships. However, since you had to conduct your review in a confidential manner (remember your confidentiality agreement), you could not divulge you were intending to buy the business. Now it is time to get in touch with the suppliers, with the assistance and support of the former owner, and introduce yourself. Business relationships are also personal relationships, and you want to give suppliers the opportunity to get to know you, and assure them that you will continue to be a good customer and will pay on time. In many ways suppliers are much like employees: when they hear a business has been sold, they worry about what is going to change, whether they will lose the account, and whether you will pay on time. So it is important to reassure them as well.

Customers are also part of your transition plan, and your customer introduction will vary according to the type of business you purchased. In retail businesses, the customers often are unaware that the business even changed hands unless you announce it. In B2B companies, you will need to meet with your key customers much like you did with your suppliers. Key customers will have the same concerns about change. They will want to know you will continue to be a reliable supplier, with good-quality products or services and no negative changes forthcoming. Again, this is best done with the cooperation of the seller during your training period.

Perhaps the most critical thing to do during your first one hundred days is to develop a good understanding of the cash flow of the business. If your business is a retail business, you pretty much get paid as you sell your goods, which is great. If your business is in the B2B sector, your customers are likely paying on terms that are typically net 30, meaning the check is in the mail and you will get paid in thirty to forty-five days after each transaction (note that some customers pay slowly;, make sure you look for this during due diligence). So, understanding how the cash comes in is very important, and it is also important to know how this works on a daily, weekly, and monthly basis. You also need to know how the cash flows out. What are your daily, weekly, and monthly expenses? Once you have this information, you can determine whether you are cash positive or cash negative on a daily, weekly, and monthly basis.

A business can be highly profitable and yet be cash negative for weeks at a time. For example, in a B2B services business, you pay for the labor and materials for all of your jobs, and then the money comes in when the customer pays thirty to forty-five days later. The money your business maintains in its bank account to cover these expenses is your working capital, and it is critical that you have sufficient working capital for the business to operate. We discussed this previously, and now it is time to revisit it and watch it on a weekly basis.

While we are talking about cash flow, let's discuss cash management. As the owner, it is critical that you closely watch the cash for the business; this includes checks, invoices, and accounts payable. You should sign every check, approve every purchase order, and approve every invoice from your suppliers. This is not micromanaging; it is watching your cash carefully. Likewise, you should review daily sales reports and other transactions, both to watch the cash and to better understand the business (remember the story of the office manager caught siphoning off $60,000 of orders!). You can do this in a paranoid way and really get your staff upset, as it will look like you don't trust them, or you can do it from day one, in a respectful way, and make it part of the way you do business, explaining that you just want to stay close to the business and understand how it all works. It is all in your approach.

Keep a running list of things you find that need improvement and questions you have about the business. You can't change everything at once. In fact, some things you initially think may need to be changed may later turn out to actually be a good way of doing business. Make a list of what needs to be reviewed after your first one hundred days.

You cannot know too much about your business. The most important part of your first one hundred days is to really dig in and get to understand the business. All aspects of it. Listen to your employees, customers, and suppliers. Learn as much as you can about your competitors. How are you better? How are they better? Do they have products or services you don't have? Are there markets you are not serving? While you are in training with the seller, be a sponge and soak up as much as you can about your new business and the industry in general. Ask the seller what he recommends you do to improve the company and grow it. Even if you don't agree, it is still great information.

My 100-Day Transition Check List

1. Training with the seller:

    a) Operational training: normal operating hours, on the job, day-to-day operations

    b) Meetings with the seller to discuss management, answer questions, discuss strategy

2. Employee transition plan: How and when will you be introduced to the team? Learn what each employee does, what their responsibilities are, and what they are trained for. Are employees cross-trained? Are there key employees?

3. Customer transition plan: How and when will you be introduced to your customers? Are there any special arrangements with key customers?

4. Supplier transition plan: How and when will you be introduced to your suppliers?

5. Cash management plan: Follow the money. Learn the ins and outs of the cash flow for your business. Set up systems to ensure that you review every invoice and every purchase order, and sign every check. Also set up daily reports so you can see the daily sales activity.

6. Financial relationships: Establish your banking relationship, establish terms with your suppliers, and review the terms offered to your customers.

7. To-do list: Start developing your list of things that can be improved in the future, potential opportunities, and questions. Set priorities as

to which you will address first once you have a good understanding of the business.

Chapter 20: My First Year

Your first one hundred days are complete; your training period with the seller is likely finished; now what? Over the course of the first year, you will complete the transition to your ownership and leadership and will start building your company. By now you are probably getting a good feel for the business, and yet there are still things about it you don't know. In the excitement of owning your own business, your entrepreneurial adrenaline will be pumping and your mind will be filled with new ideas, and consequently it may be tempting to go off in many different directions. You may have some great ideas about how to change the business; maybe they are good ones, maybe not. Or maybe they are good ideas that need to be refined a bit before they are implemented. You are not yet an expert in this business, so keep your mind open, stay objective, and take the time to research your ideas before you implement them and start making changes.

Let's look at three stories of new business owners after their first year. In chapter 4 we talked about the success story of John buying a commercial cleaning company; let's take a look at how he is doing after a year of owning the business.

John at the Commercial Cleaning Company, One Year Later

John was very proactive in his business. He soaked up everything he could learn from the previous owner (the seller), contacted all of his customers after he bought the business and got to know them and their needs, built a great relationship with his staff and listened to them, and was very engaged in the business. He really rolled up his sleeves and learned the business he bought from the ground up. By building excellent relationships with his customers he learned what they liked about his company and what they didn't like, he also learned about his competitors and how he could improve his business, and he discovered new services he could offer to his existing customers as well as to new customers. He waited to implement changes and new products until he had a good understanding of the business and how it worked. He also was very hands on in the day to day operation of the business which led him to catch the office manager siphoning off orders to her own shadow company, essentially embezzling over $60,000 a year in orders from his company. While this was bad news on the surface, after she was caught and fired it actually increased his earnings as this had been going on for some time while the previous owner ran the business.

John grew his business by thirty percent in just over a year and successfully expanded into new markets. His business is continuing to grow, is very profitable, and he is even considering expanding into even more markets. He is working on his exit strategy and continues to develop his business to increase both the earnings and value of the enterprise.

In chapter 9 we talked about the success story of Rick asking the right questions and buying the industrial distribution business. Let' review how he did after a year of owning the business.

Rick at the Distribution Company, One Year Later

Rick built a great relationship with the seller from their first meeting and maintained that relationship through the transaction and even after training. After a few months of the seller even came back and worked for Rick part time. Like John, Rick rolled up his sleeves and really got involved in the business. He learned it from top to bottom, met with the customers, built relationships with his key suppliers, and learned the details of how the business worked. After several months Rick made some improvements to the day to day operations which cut costs and improved his operating performance. Through the relationship he built with a manufacturer his company performed warranty service work for he landed a dealership agreement to sell their equipment which opened up new opportunities for growth. Approaching his one year anniversary things were going really well.

About a week before his one year anniversary disaster struck. A fire started accidently in one of the work areas and spread through the warehouse like a wildfire. There was nothing to do but evacuate the building. Thankfully no one was injured, but much of his inventory was destroyed and his warehouse was pretty much destroyed as well. Somehow his team of employees was able to get basic operations up and running in a few days, but since most of his inventory was gone and they were limping along. Because Rick was a good businessman he planned and managed his business, and insurance was part of his planning and management. He had just reviewed his insurance policy as part of his annual review and increased his coverage. His insurance policy covered the loss of the inventory, relocating the business and much of the other costs to get the business back in business.

While this seemed like a disaster the day it happened, in the end everything worked out very well for Rick. He relocated the business to a new building that was better suited for his business and much nicer. Also as a result of the fire Rick and his staff were forced to completely rethink their operations and processes. As it turned out they found a new way to manufacture one of their value added parts and substantially cut the manufacturing cost which increased his profits. As this part was one of their top selling products this had a big impact on his bottom line.

The fire could have easily destroyed his business along with the building. Because Rick planned and managed well he was prepared for this. He had adequate insurance and a well trained team of employees that were able to get the business back in business. In the end the business not only survived, it actually flourished and grew.

In the previous chapter, we discussed learning everything you can about your new business. Obviously this does not stop after one hundred days. You will never stop learning about your business, and right now you are in a high personal-growth mode as the business is still new to you. During your first year, dig into learning everything you can about your business. Learn the details about how it operates day to day; learn as much as you can about your customers, competitors, and suppliers. Ask your employees, customers, and suppliers for feedback and input on how to improve your business. You will be surprised what you can learn from them.

Now that you are a business owner it is time to change your reading habits. Reading books relevant to your business is a great way to increase your knowledge and understanding of your business. Management and sales books are great too, since you are both the CEO and probably the vice president of marketing as well. One thing to keep in mind is that most business books are written for huge companies, which I find fascinating since huge companies make up less than 1 percent of the business population, and businesses with less than one hundred employees are 98 percent of the population. I guess they figure only big business buys books. Many strategies for huge companies just aren't practical in your small business, so when you are looking for that next business book to read, make sure it is relevant to your business.

Now that you are getting settled into the business and getting a feel for how it runs, it's a good time to start working on a business plan. Many people think business plans have to be long and elaborate documents covering everything from sales and marketing, to operations, to product development, with highly detailed financial plans. Comprehensive business plans are necessary for large corporations. Large corporations are complex machines with many moving parts, and it takes a detailed plan to effectively document the strategy and communicate it to the management team and staff. Small businesses are not nearly so complex. The team is much smaller, and the product lines or services are usually tightly focused in a single niche. So do you need a business plan for a small business?

You may not need a comprehensive plan, but a basic plan stating your goals, setting timelines, and outlining how you will get there is a good idea. Your plan can be a simple outline in your own format and only a few pages long, or you can write a more formal plan using one of the business plan software programs that guide you through developing your plan.

Some Essential Elements Your Plan Should Have

Marketing: Review existing and past marketing materials. Will you continue with the existing marketing? What is your marketing budget for your first year? Are there opportunities to develop new customers or new markets with a new marketing plan? If you decide to increase or change advertising, what do you expect to get from it? How will you measure and track your results?

Sales: Review the sales process in place now. Are there existing customers that have more available business? Are there new customers you can target? Who will do this? When?

Customers: Are there old customers that were lost and can be won back? Are the current customers happy with your products and service? Are there prospective customers that have not been targeted or approached and should be?

Pricing: Surprisingly, business owners often leave prices unchanged for years, even when their costs increase, which erodes profit margins. This is because price increases are a difficult and painful decision, and owners are the one that will have to deliver the news to their customers. No wonder they avoid price increases. Selective price increases may be necessary and may be an opportunity to improve profit margins. This must be done very carefully and over time; you don't want your introduction to your new customers to be an immediate price increase. With that said, if a price increase is in order and your pricing will still be competitive, it should be done at the right time.

Competitors: Take a good and objective look at your competitors. What do they do better than your company? What does your company do better? Do they offer products or services that your company does not? Why do their customers use them? What would it take to win their customers' business?

Suppliers: Review your key suppliers. Are there any that are critical to your business (e.g., only one supplier for a key product, or major suppliers)? Is there an opportunity to reduce product costs through negotiations with your suppliers or by changing the way you buy products (e.g., volume pricing, or terms)? Are there new suppliers that can offer you better pricing or new products?

Financial plan: Develop a budget for the first year, with a revenue plan and expense budget. Monitor this monthly, reviewing your performance for the month and the year-to-date against your budget.

Cash flow: Although this is part of your financial plan, it is important enough to discuss separately. Make sure you have a monthly cash flow plan as part of your budget and that you are reviewing your cash flow weekly, along with your cash position and available working capital. As we discussed earlier, even if business is booming, cash flow can get tight until the invoices start getting paid as a result of high growth. This is where a line of credit is handy to have to cover the ups and downs in cash flow.

Staff training and cross-training: Training your staff builds a better business today and adds value to your business in the long term. Cross-training, which is training people to do more than one job, builds flexibility and reduces your dependence on key employees, which also builds a better business today and increases the value of the business.

Banking relationships: Developing a good banking relationship will be important in the future when you want new lines of credit or additional financing, perhaps to buy a building for the business. The obvious first step to developing a good banking relationship is to make sure your accounts are always in good standing, which means your balances are always sufficient, and you have no overdrafts or charge-backs on your credit card receipts. If you bank with one of the big banks, get to know the branch manager or operations manager when you open your accounts and by stopping in for deposits periodically. If you bank with a local or regional bank, the same applies, and it is a bit easier to get recognized. The best way to build credit with the bank is to start with a small line of credit, use it, pay it off, then use it again, and pay it off again. You will build a history of on-time payments and payoffs, and when you ask for a loan or a larger line of credit, your company will have a credit history with the bank.

Building Credit: Establishing and building credit should be part of your business plan. Using credit cards to finance your business is a bad idea in general; however, having a credit card in the company name is a good idea, as it will build credit for the company. The trick is to make sure you keep the balances under control. Don't let the balances increase and turn into long-term debt. This takes discipline, as it is tempting to pull out the credit card and charge that new laser printer or computer, or maybe even take a vacation on the company, and when the bill comes, just pay the minimum payment. Remember, you are using the corporate credit card to establish credit for the company for the future. If you run up a large credit card bill, you may not be able to get that line of credit or loan in the future. Your plan for credit should be to use it to float the company through the normal ups and downs of cash flow cycles or planned expansions. You have to be careful you do not use it to finance overspending or ongoing losses. If you get into a negative cash flow situation, credit is a quick fix and band aid; it will not solve the problem, so you must ensure that you address the root cause of the problem.

When you are near the end of your first year, review the results. How did revenue (sales) do with respect to your plan? Were expenses on track? Did you accomplish the goals you set for the first year? Go through your plan or budget and mark it up, making notes of what the actual results were versus the plan or goal. After you finish this and have had some time to consider the actual results, start working on your plan for your second year. This should be an annual project for you as the owner. Some owners go on a planning retreat so they can get away from the distractions of the business, think about the future, plan for the next year, and get some well-earned time off at the same time. When you get back from your planning retreat, you will have your plan for next year and be excited about starting the new year.

Chapter 21: My Exit Strategy

You just bought your business. One would think that the last thing to be thinking about is selling it. Au contraire, new entrepreneur. Now is the time to start planning. Preparing for the eventual sale from early on will build a better business today and a more valuable and marketable business in the future. By doing things right today, you are building the value of your business for the future. Developing an exit strategy is a book in itself, and I am planning to write a book on developing an exit strategy. For now, however, I will cover the basics and give you enough information to start preparing for the eventual sale of your business.

Your exit strategy can be part of your business plan (i.e., a section of your business plan) or can be a separate document. In developing your exit strategy, the first step is to envision what the business is going to look like when you sell it, and then outline how you intend to get it there. Some questions to ask yourself when you are thinking about this are: What will the annual sales be? What products and services will we be offering? (Note: it is OK to stay in the same niche.) What will the staff be like? And most importantly, what is my time line? Perhaps the most important thing to understand about any plan, whether it is a business plan or exit strategy, is that these are living documents. By this I mean that the plans will evolve and change along with the business. As you learn more about the business, you will likely change both the business plan and exit strategy. Likewise, new opportunities will arise, and the business itself will likely evolve and change, which will again drive a change in the business plan and exit strategy. The point is that these are not static documents that are written once, filed away, and forgotten. These are living documents that will change along with the business over time. This is one very good reason to keep the plan simple, so it will be easy to update and not an overwhelming project.

Things to Do Today to Increase the Value of Your Business

1. Books and records: Keep in mind what you were looking for in books and records when you were looking for a business as a buyer. Make sure the P&Ls are complete, make sense, and document the financial performance of the business accurately. Document your

owner benefits consistently, so when it is time to recast your P&L to determine the DE, it will be easy to do and easy to verify during due diligence.

2. Focus on profitability and growth: By now you understand well that earnings drive value. Every dollar you add to your bottom line and DE adds two to three dollars to the value of your business.

3. Staff: Ensure that your staff is well-trained and cross-trained if possible. Build a solid and stable team capable of running the day-to-day operations.

4. Dependency on you as the owner: Build the business so it will be easy for a buyer to take over. Remember your concerns about taking over the owner's role; build your business today so it will be easy for someone else to replace you in the future. This will involve procedures documenting how things are done, a good staff, and a well-run business in general.

5. Dependency on a single customer or a few customers: If you have any single customer that represents over 20 percent of your business, work on expanding and diversifying your customer base.

6. Dependency on a single or a few suppliers: If you have a single supplier or a few suppliers that are critical to your business, work on ways to reduce this dependency. In some businesses, this is not possible. If that's the case for your business, ensure that your suppliers and your relationships with them are rock solid and transferrable to a buyer.

7. Procedures and documentation: Documenting how things are done makes it easy to train new staff and easier for a buyer to step in later.

8. Tax planning: Surprisingly few business owners sit down with their CPA to plan for the eventual sale or transfer of the business. Even if you plan to transfer the business to your children, in fact especially if you intend to do this, you need to plan for this. When you sell or otherwise transfer the business, there will be taxes to be paid. These taxes can be minimized if you plan in advance and do things properly. Meet with your CPA to develop an exit strategy that will minimize the taxes when you sell or transfer the business. Even if you don't have a specific time line, you can lay the proper foundation today to minimize your taxes when you transfer the business.

Developing your exit strategy is a task that is easy to postpone. Obviously, if you don't develop your exit strategy in your second year, the business would continue to operate as usual and would not be harmed in the short term. Here is the problem with procrastinating on the development of your exit strategy: if not now, when? There will never be a great time to develop your exit strategy. You will always be busy, there will always be urgent issues requiring your attention, and it will always seem like next month or next year would be a better time. Ask yourself this question: are these short-term tasks and issues worth paying double the taxes and perhaps sacrificing the future value of your business? Your exit strategy is for you. It is your plan to maximize the value of your business, minimize your taxes, and ultimately achieve the goal you bought the business for—building your future. So take the time to plan for your future. You owe it to yourself and your family.

Afterword

We have covered a great deal of material, and I sincerely hope you found the material useful, informative, and perhaps even inspiring. Buying a business truly is the beginning of the journey to building your future; it can be a fun journey, albeit a very challenging one at times, but in the end, it will be rewarding in many ways. In addition to financial gains, you will certainly experience a great deal of personal growth over the course of looking for a business, buying it, and then running it. In doing this you will go from dreaming about becoming a successful entrepreneur to being one. With this success comes responsibility. As a business owner you will have the unique opportunity to lead and inspire others: your employees, customers, and suppliers. You will also have the opportunity to give back to your community in a variety of ways. Many miss these opportunities, not realizing the gifts they have to give, as they are too wrapped up in the day-to-day grind trying to get just a little bit more done and make a little more money.

There are many measures for success; the most important have no monetary value. In the end, the measure of your success will be more than the dollar figure on the balance sheet of your business; it will be measured by the balance sheet of your life. How you led others, how you shared your knowledge and experience, how you maintained your personal integrity, the example you set and live by, and the lives you touch along the way; through these seemingly small things, you can have a significant impact on many people.

Rick Warren, senior pastor of Saddleback Church and author of *The Purpose Driven Life*, once said in a sermon, you can live a life chasing success or live a life of significance; the choice is yours. This is a profound point. I leave you with that to ponder and sincerely hope you achieve success and live a generous life of significance.

Abbreviations

401k: Retirement investment plan (see glossary)

A/P: Accounts Payable

A/R: Accounts Receivable

B2B: Business to Business

B2C: Business to Consumer

CPA: Certified Public Accountant

COE: Close of Escrow

COGS: Cost of Goods Sold

COP: Change of Possession

DBA: Doing Business As

DE: Discretionary Earnings

DTI: Debt to Income ratio

EBIT: : Earnings Before Interest & Taxes

EBITDA: Earnings Before Interest Taxes Depreciation & Amortization

ERSOP: Entrepreneur Rollover Stock Ownership Plan

FDD: Franchise Disclosure Document

FFE: Furniture Fixtures & Equipment

FSBO: For Sale By Owner

FTC: Federal Trade Commission

GDP: Gross Domestic Product

HELOC: Home Equity Line of Credit

IFA: International Franchise Association

LLC: Limited Liability Company

LTV: Loan to Value

M&A: Mergers and Acquisitions

NOL: Net Operating Loss

P&L: Profit & Loss

QSR: Quick Service Restaurant

ROI: Return on Investment

SBA: Small Business Administration

SDC: Seller's Discretionary Cash, see DE

SDCF: Seller's Discretionary Cash Flow, see DE

SDE: Seller's Discretionary Earnings, see DE

SWOT: Strengths Weaknesses Opportunities and Threats

IRA: Individual Retirement Account

IRS: Internal Revenue Service

W2: Tax form prepared by the employer showing the employees annual wages.

Glossary of General Terms and Definitions

7a loan: An SBA (U.S. Small Business Administration) loan for the acquisition of a business. A 7a loan presently has a cap of $2 million. Various bills have been proposed in Congress to increase this cap to $3 million, but have not passed as of this publication.

401k: A retirement investment plan where the employee contributes a percentage of earned wages into a tax-deferred investment account selected by the employer.

504 loan: An SBA loan for the acquisition of capital equipment or real estate for a business. The cap for 504 loans is $7 million.

add-back: Add-backs are the owner's discretionary and personal expenses that are added back to the businesses operating expenses to arrive at the discretionary earnings, or DE. See chapter 10 for a complete explanation and example.

amortization: This is the recovery of the cost of an investment in intangible assets, such as a franchise agreement, or licensing over a period of time. For example, a $40,000 investment in a franchise agreement amortized over ten years would result in annual amortization of $4,000.

adjustment: see add-back

accounts payable (A/P): These are the invoices to the company from its suppliers that are owed to the suppliers.

accounts receivable (A/R): These are the amounts owed to the company by customers that have been invoiced for goods delivered or services performed. In most cases, invoices are due in thirty days.

business broker: A person specializing in the sale of small to midsize businesses.

cash flow: Cash flow is a financial term that is often misapplied, and some confuse it with DE. The correct definition of cash flow is the net cash flow from operations of a business. This is literally the cash the business put in the bank at the end of the month after paying expenses. It is seldom the same as the profit shown on your profit and loss statement, or P&L, as the P&L may have depreciation and amortization shown on it, and also may show expenses or income that were not actually paid during the month (depending upon whether you are using cash or accrual accounting).

cost of goods sold (COGS): This is the cost of the products sold by the company (e.g., materials plus labor). Labor costs included in this figure vary, depending on how the certified public accountant, or CPA, treats labor on the P&L.

comparable sales (also known as "comps"): Data from sales of similar types and sizes of businesses. The typical figures used are a multiple of DE and a percentage of gross earnings.

contingency: Conditions that must be met in order for the transaction to move forward to the next step.

contingency removal: This is when you formally approve one of the conditions (contingencies) specified in your offer, such as due diligence, equipment inspection, lease, and financing. Also see passive contingency removal.

corporation: See entity.

discretionary earnings (DE): The owner's total economic benefit from the business. Also known as SDE or SDC. See chapter 10 for a complete explanation and example.

depreciation: This recaptures the investment in equipment, property, and other assets over a period of time. For example, a $25,000 investment depreciated over five years would result in depreciation of $5,000 per year for five years. Depreciation is commonly referred to as a "write-off."

due diligence: This is the review and inspection of the business by the buyer to verify the quality of the business, the earnings, and the claims by the seller.

earnings: This can mean a number of things. Net profit, EBITDA, and DE are all earnings. When discussing earnings, make sure you know which figure is being referred to.

entity: In business, the form the business is held in is referred to as an entity. Business entities can be corporations, LLCs, sole proprietorships, or partnerships.

escrow: Escrow is a neutral third party used in many states to hold and distribute the funds for the transaction and process the transaction documents.

intermediary: A person facilitating the sale of small to midsize businesses, including M&A transactions of privately held businesses.

lien: A lien is the document filed with the county or state where the assets of the business are held by a lender as collateral, or in same cases as the result of a judgment or other debt.

note: A note, also known as a promissory note, is the document used for a loan from the seller (in this case the lender) to the buyer, providing financing for part of the purchase price.

passive contingency removal: This is a clause or sentence stating that contingencies are deemed removed by the buyer after the contingency date has passed and at the close of escrow. These are usually related to due diligence and review of equipment or the business. Be very careful of these if they are in your purchase offer or contract, as you can unknowingly lose contingencies if you do not notify the broker otherwise before the date. If your purchase offer or contract has a passive contingency removal in it, make sure you write an addendum or amendment stating that all contingencies must be removed in writing by the buyer.

profit: This term can actually have several meanings. There is gross profit, pretax profit, and net profit, as well as EBITDA, DE, and the very broad term of "earnings." When someone is using the term "profit," make sure you know which figure they are referring to.

SBA: The U.S. Small Business Administration provides guaranties for small business loans in order to provide liquidity to the small business market and facilitate the growth of small business. The SBA is not a lender and not a bank. The SBA provides approved SBA lenders with loan guarantees for loans that meet the SBA criteria.

SDE: See DE above.

seller note: A note, also known as a promissory note, used for a loan from the seller (in this case the lender) to the buyer, providing financing for part of the purchase price.

transaction (deal): The term "transaction" is often used to refer to the sale or purchase of a business. The term "deal" is also often used.

valuation: This typically refers to a formal calculation of the value of the company. Third-party valuations are independent valuations prepared by a business analyst and are similar to an appraisal for real estate. Brokers and intermediaries often prepare market value valuations, which while less rigorous, are sufficient for small businesses if done correctly. See chapter 11 for more information on valuation.

working capital: This is the cash required to operate the company on a daily or monthly basis. The amount of working capital required varies widely depending on the size and type of company.

Appendix 1: Financial Ratios and Terms

cap rate or capitalization rate: the cap rate equals DE less replacement salary, divided by the total purchase price. Note that this does not include debt service. Subtract a manager's salary, equivalent salary, or the salary you are giving up from the DE and then divide this by the total purchase price.

cash-on-cash return: Cash-on-cash return equals DE less debt service, divided by the down payment. This is a measure of how quickly your cash investment is returned. Transactions with leveraging (financing) will have much higher cash-on-cash returns, as less cash is injected into the transaction.

debt to income ratio (DTI): DTI equals DE less replacement salary, divided by total debt service. Most lenders want this figure to be higher than 1.2, and some prefer 1.25. For example, if the DE for a business is $200,000, your replacement salary is $100,000, and the annual debt service is $80,000, then DTI = ($200,000 – $100,000) / $80,000 = 1.25. This means that the business generates 25 percent more cash after your salary than the debt service. If the DTI was 100 percent, this would mean that all of the income after your salary would be used to service the debt, and that there is no excess cash for contingencies or extraordinary expenses, which explains why the banks want a DTI of at least 1.2.

return on investment (ROI): ROI equals DE divided by total investment; for the purchase of a business, this is DE divided by the total purchase price.

Appendix 2: Sample Due Diligence Items for Midsize Businesses

The due diligence list below is an informational sample of some of the items you may want to review during due diligence. Keep in mind that in some cases the company you are looking at legitimately may not have some of these items, as many small businesses have limited books and records. Likewise, there may be additional items you need to request and review that are unique to the business you are looking at. There is no "universal" due diligence list. The information necessary to successfully and thoroughly verify the financial and business condition of a company varies with each business. Your objective in due diligence is to confirm the financial and operational condition of the company to your satisfaction before moving forward with the transaction. Review your due diligence list with your CPA, attorney, and broker prior to submitting it to the seller.

1. Financial information: Last three years' tax returns, last three years' P&L and balance sheets, A/R report showing account aging , A/P (accounts payable) report, monthly and year-end bank statements for the last twelve months, selected review of invoices to customers, selected review of purchase orders, general ledger, payroll tax returns, sales tax returns, owner's W2s for the last three years, breakdown and documentation of seller's add-backs and benefits.

2. Sales reports: In addition to the financial reports, sales reports by product line or service, by month and by year, are very informative if the company has this level of detail. Some of these reports may also show the gross margin by product line or service as well.

3. Business contracts: Review contracts with suppliers (e.g., distribution contracts), contracts, if any, with customers, and contracts for services (e.g., phone, equipment, maintenance). In some cases, there may be contracts in the seller/owner's name and the company is incorporated. Technically, the contract is not with the company; it is with the individual. If this is the case, make sure the contracts are included in your purchase agreement (specifically) and that they are

transferred to you in the purchase. You may need a separate purchase agreement or amendment to your purchase agreement to deal with this; check with your broker and attorney if this pops up.

4. Liens, loans, debts, leases: Obtain a copy of any liabilities, such are liens, loans/debts, and leases. You want to ensure that these are paid off by the seller. Also, if you are assuming a lease for equipment, you want to make sure you understand the terms and whether it is indeed transferable (many are not).

5. Lease: Review the lease, meet with the landlord, and discuss what your terms will be. Will it be a new lease or an assignment of the existing lease? Ask if there is a transfer fee involved, and find out who is paying for it (sorry, usually it is the buyer, but you can ask anyway). Also, find out what the seller's security deposit is, as you will be assuming this and reimbursing the seller, and whether your security deposit will be increased.

6. Corporate records: Articles of incorporation and amendments, board meeting minutes, list of shareholders, certificate from secretary of state, and tax ID.

7. Insurance policies: Review the current insurance policies and claims for the last three years.

8. Seller disclosure statement: The broker may have one, or you can use one from your attorney or the one from *http://www.mybusinessbroker. com.*

9. Litigation: Ask (in writing; it should be part of the seller disclosure statement) if there has been any litigation in the past, if there is any pending, and if there is any anticipated.

10. Sales and product information: Sales literature, product specifications, production procedures, etc. Review the products and services you are buying.

11. Inventory report: Breakdown of inventory by item, with costing, turnover (sales activity), and aging.

12. Customer list: A complete list of all past and current customers of the business. Some sellers may be reluctant to provide the actual names of the customers early on, and this often becomes a point of contention, as you need this information to verify the condition of the business. In some cases you may be able to verify this with the customer names removed and replaced with numbers, allowing you to match invoices with payments to verify the customers are indeed

active, and to review their historical activity. Another way to resolve this is with an additional confidentiality agreement.

13. Staff/employees: List of employees, review employee records (if available), confirm I9 (immigration status), pay levels and history, performance reviews (few small businesses actually document this), etc.

14. FFE (furniture, fixtures, and equipment): Detailed equipment list, verify condition, confirm equipment is owned or leased. If equipment is leased, review the lease agreement and the terms. You want to make sure the lease isn't expiring soon and that you won't either lose the equipment or get stuck with any fees for purchasing the equipment. If the equipment is owned, make sure the purchase agreement includes all owned equipment.

15. Licenses and permits: Check the applicable licenses and permits, including city and state, and check federal and state tax IDs. Make sure the name on the permits is correct and that the address is correct; most importantly, make sure the business has the appropriate licenses and permits and that they are still valid.

16. Fictitious name filings (also known as DBA, or "doing business as"): Basically you are ensuring that the seller has a legal right to use the name being used, and that the name will be transferred to you. This should be in your purchase agreement.

17. Trademarks: Many small businesses don't bother to register trademarks. If they have a trademark, verify that they indeed own the rights to it, and more importantly make sure the trademark is transferred to you when you buy the business. In some cases the trademark may be owned by an individual (the seller/owner) and the business may be incorporated. If this is the case, make sure the owner of the trademark transfers ownership to you and that it is included in the sale.

18. Patents: Patents are even less common than trademarks in small businesses. If the business has one, make sure it is transferred to you when you purchase the business. Also, find out who owns the patent rights, and make sure the owner transfers the rights to you along with the sale.

Bibliography

1. Epstein, Lita. *Reading Financial Reports For Dummies.* New Jersey: Wiley Publishing, Inc., 2004.

2. Headd, Brian. 2003. Redefining business success: Distinguishing between closure and failure. *Small Business Economics* 21: March 51–61.

3. International Franchise Association. *Consumer Guide to Buying a Franchise.* Available at *www.franchise.org/franchiseesecondary.aspx?amp;langtype=1033&id=10002*

4. IRS Revenue Ruling 59-60. Available at *www.irs.gov*

5. Pratt, Shannon P., Robert F. Reilly, and Robert P. Schweihs. *Valuing Small Businesses and Professional Practices.* 3rd ed. New York: McGraw-Hill Professional, 1998.

6. Robb, Russell. *Buying Your Own Business.* Massachusetts: Adams Media Corporation, 1995.

7. Rust, H. Lee. *Let's Buy a Company.* New Jersey: The Career Press, 2006.

8. Tracy, John. *How to Read a Financial Report: Wringing Vital Signs Out of the Numbers.* New Jersey: Wiley & Sons, 2004.

9. Tauli, Tom. *The Complete M&A Handbook.* California: Prima Publishing, 2002.

10. U.S. Census Bureau. Data and statistics about United States Business Size (including Small Business) from the United States Census Bureau and Bureau of Labor Statistics, data from 2002 and 2004 reports. Available at *www.census.gov*

11. U.S. Department of Labor. "Small Business and Self Employment for People with Disabilities." 2000. www.dol.gov/odep/archives/ek00/small.htm.

12. U.S. Federal Trade Commission. *Buying a Franchise: A Consumer Guide.* Available at *www.ftc.gov/bcp/edu/pubs/consumer/invest/inv05.shtm*

13. U.S Small Business Administration. *Basic 7a Loan Program.* Available at *www.sba.gov/services/financialassistance/sbaloantopics/7a/*

14. U.S. Small Business Administration. "The Small Business Economy For Data Year 2006: A Report to the President." 2007. www.sba.gov/advo/research/sb_econ2007.pdf.

Endorsements

"Rarely do you come across a book that provides hands-on practical advice in every chapter. Bill's real-life experiences as an entrepreneur, CEO, and business broker leave the reader with a blueprint for business acquisitions. Ivory tower theory is not going to go a long way in an acquisition; one needs to get down in the trenches, as Bill explains chapter by chapter."

Karl Fava, President, Business Financial Consultants, Inc.

"I couldn't recommend a more salient primer for persons interested in purchasing a business. Bill Grunau distills the complexities of the purchase and sale of businesses into a plain English and common-sense format that will allow inexperienced buyers or sellers to confidently spot and navigate potential minefields in the transaction. Undoubtedly, the book can allow its reader to make better decisions—ones that will lead to successful results, profitability, and peace of mind!"

Thomas Lombardi, founding partner, Palmer, Lombardi, and Donohue, LLP, law firm

"Bill's polished style of writing reflects a common-sense approach to buyer and seller concerns through the acquisition and divestiture process. A must-read for first-time buyers and sellers of privately held businesses."

Glenn Haddad, Corporate Trainer and Business Intermediary with over twenty years of experience